The View Through the Medicine Wheel

Shamanic maps of how

the Universe works

First published by O Books, 2008
O Books is an imprint of John Hunt Publishing
Ltd., The Bothy, Deershot Lodge, Park Lane,
Ropley, Hants, SO24 0BE, UK
office1@o-books.net
www.o-books.net

Distribution in:

UK and Europe
Orca Book Services
orders@orcabookservices.co.uk
Tel: 01202 665432 Fax: 01202 666219 Int. code
(44)

USA and Canada
NBN
custserv@nbnbooks.com
Tel: 1 800 462 6420 Fax: 1 800 338 4550

Australia and New Zealand
Brumby Books
sales@brumbybooks.com.au
Tel: 61 3 9761 5535 Fax: 61 3 9761 7095

Far East (offices in Singapore, Thailand, Hong
Kong, Taiwan)
Pansing Distribution Pte Ltd
kemal@pansing.com
Tel: 65 6319 9939 Fax: 65 6462 5761

South Africa
Alternative Books
altbook@peterhyde.co.za
Tel: 021 555 4027 Fax: 021 447 1430

Text copyright Leo Rutherford 2008

Design: Stuart Davies

Cover artwork: Howard G. Charing

ISBN: 978 1 84694 108 5

A CIP catalogue record for this book is available
from the British Library.

Printed in the UK by CPI Antony Rowe

O Books operates a distinctive and ethical publishing philosophy in
all areas of its business, from its global network of authors to
production and worldwide distribution.
This book is produced on FSC certified stock, within ISO14001
standards. The printer plants sufficient trees each year through
the Woodland Trust to absorb the level of emitted carbon in
its production.

The View Through the Medicine Wheel

Shamanic maps of how

the Universe works

Leo Rutherford

BOOKS

Winchester, UK
Washington, USA

CONTENTS

THANKS

Thanks first to all those indigenous people who kept the ancient medicine alive against the most appalling persecution from the invaders who stole their lands, took their livelihood, made them foreigners in their own countries and forced their cockeyed religious beliefs upon them.

Thanks to all those who taught me patiently and helped me recover my-self from the brainwashing of my own culture, its religions and education.

Thanks to all my friends and co-workers through *Eagle's Wing*, especially Dawn Russell and Lorraine Grayston, who have contributed so much to my life, and therefore to this book.

Thanks to my friend Karen Kent who helped me edit this manuscript into a better order and to John Hunt & O Books who published it.

PREFACE

I went to live in the San Francisco Bay Area in 1977 when I was in the midst of a mid-life crisis. I went in desperation to find a way of healing myself. Thirty years later I find myself pursuing a whole way of life and career that is far from anything I could have imagined. Far from the world of manufacturing industry where I spent my first twenty working years, I find myself following a much more ancient profession than engineering and industrial management - that of travelling medicine man. I had thought that I entered a 'new' age only to find myself involved in something exceedingly ancient.

The Medicine Wheel teachings did more than anything else to help me re-frame my world, to see and feel the world from a holistic point of view as a tapestry of interlinking forces and powers. The teachings helped me to form a mental web into which I could fit all my experiences and all the diverse and variegated bits and pieces of myself that had previously warred with each other. Previously I had always found 'God' at odds with sexuality; the religious need to believe all sorts of unlikely historical events in order to be 'saved' at odds with common sense and a practical measure of skepticism; my desires to be myself in the world at odds with teachings about spiritual matters that seemed to call for only retreat and meditation; group psychotherapy which taught about expressing one's truth freely all the time at odds with the need for a degree of stealth and cunning in everyday matters..... In a word, my inner landscape was something of a quagmire. With the guidance of the medicine wheel I was able to put many things into correct relationship and shed great light on what was really going on in my life. Furthermore it gave me a life map, a way of seeing not another belief system that depended on accepting all sorts of unproven and un-provable dogmas. It was a way to knowledge that helped and guided me to make sense of my fragmented inner self and of my actual experiences of life.

My first experience of Native American teachings was a workshop with Hyemeyohsts Storm and his then apprentice, Harley Swiftdeer, back in the late 70's in the San Francisco Bay Area where I was living at the time. It was a very pleasant and stimulating day that encouraged me to seek more, and shortly after I participated in a weekend on self mastery with Doug Boyd, a long-term apprentice of the medicine man, Rolling Thunder. In June of 1978, I took part in the first of many workshops with the wonderful movement teacher Gabrielle Roth. She called her dance work 'shamanic' and she most certainly imbibes the spirit of shamanism. Two years later when Joan Halifax came to Antioch University where I was then studying for my MA in Holistic Psychology in an extraordinary programme created by Will Schutz, I was fully turned on to this path for life. Joan gave a five-day-long course and brought these ancient ways and teachings alive and relevant for me here and now in this technological, 'developed', world. The innate wisdom and knowledge of the earth and life was inescapable. The breadth of understanding of the challenges and struggles of being human was a revelation. It helped me to align my mind much more with the cosmos instead of approaching life as if it were a booby-trapped battle with nature, 'God', and other people.

I continued learning about the Medicine Wheel with Harley Swiftdeer while I was living in California but on my return to England in 1982, I was unable to pursue further study. It was not until 1986 that my friend Heather Campbell brought Swiftdeer to England and I continued studying avidly with him in that and the following year. Also in 1986 I travelled to Peru for a very enlightening journey with don Eduardo Calderon, Inca shaman, and Alberto Villoldo, his apprentice at that time (and PhD San Francisco University lecturer/teacher). This journey was based around the Inca understanding of the medicine wheel. I studied further with Joan Halifax when she visited England in the late 80's and when I took a group to Mexico in '92 for a journey with her group to the sacred sites of Chiapas. I further studied with Hyemeyohsts Storm when he visited the UK in 1996 & 1997.

This book is about what I have come to understand through working with and teaching the Medicine Wheels for more than 20 years. It is culled from study, personal process and insights gained through the teachings and reflections. It therefore comes to you with a white western British accent, not from an indigenous author, though I am most certainly indigenous to Planet Earth. This is not intended to be an 'authentic' work of a native shaman but a work of exploration by someone from Western-middle-class culture whose life has been transformed from exposure to these teachings.

The industrialised cultures have lost much of their connection to Mother Earth and to their actual roots, and are damaging the fabric of the planet with technological 'advancement'. The white Christianised races have grown up being told what to believe rather than being given guidance to find out what is true, told how to behave rather than encouraged and guided to find out what behaviour brings happiness and contentment, and this has left a vacuum of understanding and great ignorance of how the Universe really works. I suffered quite enormously from this misguidance and ignorance and I write as someone who has found a path to walk out of the darkness of confusion and into the light of understanding. A process, I stress, that is ongoing. I therefore see myself as having a bridging role in bringing these ancient ways to modern people and translating them into language which is understandable to urban and suburban people.

My primary teachers and sources for this material are Hyemeyohsts Storm, whose wonderful book 'Lightningbolt' includes many teachings of the wheel; Harley Swiftdeer who teaches and spreads the knowledge through the Deer Tribe Medicine Society; and Joan Halifax who brings together Buddhism and the Medicine Way through the Upaya Foundation. My gratitude to them. Addresses are in the resource list.

My hope is that I have been able to conjure the Medicine Wheels to speak to you directly themselves. If so, then the magic is all theirs.

INTRODUCTION

WHAT IS THE MEDICINE WHEEL?

The Medicine Wheel is a circle of power and knowledge, a way of understanding life, framed in a circle. It teaches of our connection to all things, it shows us our way back to Centre, our way home. The Medicine Wheel is a reflection of the Universe and the individual. As above, so below - the greater is reflected in the lesser and the lesser in the greater.

The Medicine Wheel is not a belief system but a way to see life more clearly, a series of maps to help understand the structure of life and see how one action causes another. It teaches how to steer a good heart-full road through life's many challenging and variegated circumstances.

The ancient matriarchal cultures saw their world in terms of circles and cycles and so it was natural that they should teach of life in this manner. The Jewish Kabbalah is another way of teaching essential truths but presented in a vertical format as befits a more masculine oriented society. Each system comes from the understandings and attitudes of its culture of origin and none is better or worse, they are merely different ways of understanding life on earth.

WHAT IS THE MEANING OF 'MEDICINE'?
Medicine means vital force, life force, wholeness. To be whole is to be healed, to bring to an end the separation of the parts of oneself and separation from life so as to become a fully integrated human. A fully integrated whole human is a holy person.

Medicine is anything which brings personal power and understanding, strength and wisdom gained through life experience. Medicine is power in the real sense of that word - power over oneself and one's ability to respond to and to consciously co-create life.

The Medicine Wheel teaches the living of life in a way that

brings healing and health to the Earth Mother and to all of our family, friends, and fellow creatures. It guides us to maintain our connection to the Great Mystery and to all aspects of life. Our *Personal Medicine* is what we have to 'give-away' to other humans and to the world. It is what we contribute to the collective in our lifetime. It is what we can look back on at the end of life with pride and pleasure - what we gave to the evolution of All-That-Is, our unique contribution to the evolution of All Life.

WHERE DOES THE MEDICINE WHEEL COME FROM?

Medicine Wheel teachings have come down to us from the ancient cultures in all parts of the world. All over the world can be found the remnants of stone circles.

The systems of Wheels we will be studying in this book originate in Central America, most probably the Mayan culture, though it is not easy to tell just what their furthest origins are.

There are many systems of Medicine Wheel teachings in many differing forms from different parts of the world, with the Elements and Powers often placed in quite different directions. The particular direction is not important in itself as the teachings are about relationship. Each Medicine Wheel system is complete and usually cannot be mixed with another system, though the teachings are always complementary and similar.

WHAT IS IT FOR?

The Medicine Wheel is a way of teaching fundamental truths about our world. It is not didactic and it is not a belief system but a path to knowledge, a way of 'seeing' the Universe and its great powers, of understanding our individual place in the scheme of things, and learning about the relationships of these powers to each other and to ourselves. These teachings have come to us from our ancestors who learned them through experience. It is for us to test them by our own experience and make them live for us.

WHAT WILL THE STUDY TEACH ME?

How we frame our world is very important.

THE UNIVERSE WORKS LIKE A HALL OF MIRRORS.
That may sound a fantastical statement. If so, I hope that by the
end of this book it will make complete and utter sense to you. The
point is that what we 'see' depends on our frame of reference, what
we allow ourselves to see, on how we look at things. There is a
story about some indigenous people in South America asking
newly arrived sailors 'How did you get here? 'On that ship' they
replied pointing to their galley anchored in the bay. The local
people were unable to 'see' the ship, it was not in their frame of
reference, and it was only when they had been out and walked
upon it, touched it and experienced it for themselves, that they
were able to accept its existence. We are all like that. We tend not
to 'see' things until we are ready for them. This study will help
broaden your frame of reference and enable you to 'see' more.

THE DIRECTIONS AND THEIR POWERS
There are four cardinal directions - and the Centre makes five.
Then there is the Above and the Below, and that makes seven.
Seven is the number of the *Dream* of the Creator in manifestation.
It is the Creator experiencing him/her/itself. The Medicine Wheel
is a path towards understanding the Creator's 'Dream' and the
multitude of powers that affect our life in the third dimension of
material reality.

Here is an introduction to the powers of the four directions.

POWERS OF THE EAST
The East of the Wheel is where the sun rises. It is the place of begin-
nings and endings, of vision and inspiration - where spirit comes
into matter and where matter touches spirit - the place that is
beyond the confines of linear time. It is springtime and the
planting of seeds and the beginning of sprouting.

It is the place of the myths of Eagle and Condor who fly
between the worlds and see the big picture from high above. It is
the place of the Mage, of 'I-mage-a-nation' where we learn that
what we imagine can become real-ised. It is the place of the
visionary, the one who sees beyond the apparent reality, and of the

energy matrix which underlies the physical bodies of all living things. It is the high place where we can go to be alone and to contemplate Life, the Universe and Everything.

It is the Fire of Spirit where dross gets burned away and where we need to navigate with care to make sure it is only the dross and not ourselves that gets burned. It is the place of the Mens' Council and of the Heyeokah, the contrary-joker-comedian who teaches truth through showing the world upside down.

POWERS OF THE SOUTH

The South of the Wheel is the place of trust and innocence, the time of childhood. It is the place of emotion, energy-motion, of water and of the heart. We learn to touch and be touched, to feel and to be moved by the beauty and magic of the world. The South is where the child experiences the world as alive, shimmering and connected.

South is the place where time begins for us and later, in adult life, it is the place where our past experiences affect our present until we turn the mirror-of-self-reflection upon ourselves. South is the place of White Buffalo Woman who brings the Medicine Pipe to the people to teach and remind us of the sacredness of all things.

There is a medicine teaching which says we can look at spiritual childhood as lasting until we are about 27, just before (in astrology) Saturn returns and turns lives upside down.

POWERS OF THE WEST

The West is the place of the setting sun where we draw ourselves inwards to do inner work. This is woman's place, the deep, the dark, the womb where new creation is nurtured, the 'looks-within' place. The West is the place of Grandmother Earth who gives life and who teaches of cycles and patience, of the permanence of change, of death, decay and rebirth, and that Death-Gives-Life and all things are born, live, die, decay and give new life. It is the direction of all things physical, of the now, the present moment which is the only time that physical matter knows.

West is the place of Bear who hibernates for the long winter and dreams; of Owl who knows the night; and of Jaguar who teaches of death and the need to overcome inertia, deadness, and become a Spiritual Warrior who knows that all 'enemies' are really allies and teachers.

It is the place of the Inner Spiritual Being of opposite polarity, woman's Inner Man and man's Inner Woman, who we make contact with when we shut out the stimulus of the outer world and touch the silence within.

This is the place of our spiritual adolescence, which can be looked on as the period from around 27 to 54 years of age, the time of apparent maturity in the everyday world during which we are working through adolescence in our inner world.

POWERS OF THE NORTH

The North is the place of winter when the ground is frozen and we have to learn to co-operate to survive. It is where we learn to achieve adulthood with maturity and to giveaway to one another, and that the survival of the tribe, group, village, country or planet is more important than that of any one individual. This is where we learn to plan for the future and to look at how our actions will affect the next seven generations that follow us.

The North is the place of the wind, of mind, of thinking, of intellect. The animal totems are the Great White Buffalo who gives all of himself to feed and clothe the people and so teaches of the sacredness of the giveaway and reminds us that we, in our turn, give away all we have 'borrowed' from Mother Earth at the end of our time here. Also Wolf who is teacher, direction finder and keeper of the family; Horse who is keeper of wisdom and philosophy, and Dragon who leads us to an encounter with direct knowing, a face-to-face encounter with power.

North is the place of mystery teachings such as the Medicine Wheel, the ancient ways of the shaman, teachings of what it means to become fully human (*Hu* means divine, *man* means mortal). Adulthood can be considered as the period of life from around 54 to 81 years, the time where we can gain true maturity of spirit in matter.

.... AND THEN WE RETURN TO THE EAST.

And so as our life comes towards its completion we come back once more to the East, now as an elder. We can think of this as the period from about 81 years to 108, or whenever we are called from this life. This is when we return to the simplicity of childhood as our outer faculties lessen and we move more inward, back towards our essential being, the spirit-self who came in at the beginning. All of life leads to death. It is a circle. The teachings say that linear time is an illusion which we experience in the third dimension only. That means that we will step back into the spirit world at the same moment that we left it to come into this world. From Spirit's view, our whole life journey in the blink of an eye!

As the end of our life approaches, the fire begins to burn up the matter of our bodies until just the essence is left. The quality of our old age is dependent upon how much we have done to clear, heal and develop our-Self and our potential during our journey, on how much we have kept *in-spirit*, inspired, connected to our essence, and on how much we have done to develop our gifts and talents and to give them in service to others. In the old cultures, the elders were the Wise Ones who, through the trials and tests of life, gained immeasurably valuable life experience that they made available to the younger generations. This tradition has almost vanished in the 'developed' world - and the 'developed' world may vanish unless it returns.

Each of the directions can be considered as a 'lodge', a home. The teachings say that we will be 'at home' in one of the four directions, and its trials and tests will be easy for us. Two other directions will require work but their lessons can be learned with dedicated effort. The fourth direction, however, is where our biggest challenges will lie and it may require our lifetime's work to gain mastery of its lessons.

ENEMIES OF THE DIRECTIONS.

Each direction has its 'enemy', its corruption, it's self-glorification:

East: Spiritual pride, power over others, rejection of the Earth and matter and attachment to 'superior spiritual affairs'.

South: Self pity, 'pain games', lack of responsibility, child-ishness.

West: Self obsession, inertia (deadness while alive), depression, fear of death.

North: Knowledge without wisdom, intellectual arrogance, dogma, pedantry, beliefs without experience; the critical, judgmental mind that destroys the self while it thinks it is cleverly showing superiority over others.

THE PLACE OF BALANCE

In this realm of duality no force can exist without its opposite. There must be good for us to know bad and bad for us to know good. When we come to the centre, the place of balance, the centre of the cross, the centre of the wheel of our life, we can hold these forces together in harmony. It is our life task to balance these forces within ourselves and so to steer ourselves through the Great Maze of manifest life.

Each one of us has our own particular journey to travel and each one of us has to make our own decisions at every turn. In childhood there are parents and Father-Christmas figures to guide and take responsibility for us. Once into adulthood there is no one there, no Big-Daddy-in-the-Sky Father-Christmas God-like replacement, nothing except our-Self. We have spirit guides and ancestors who may guide but do not take responsibility for us. The journey is one of making our own way, through our own choices and our own effort, and of taking responsibility for the outcome. No one is to blame, there is no blame, there is just experience to be experienced and awareness, perception and consciousness to be gained. Each direction is a mirror and it reflects to us what we need to know in order to grow, develop and complete our-Self. Its purpose is to help and guide us to return home to the place of balance, alignment, harmony, and health that is our Centre where our little will merges with the Great Will of Creation. Ho!

PROLOGUE

THE COSMOS

IN THE BEGINNING -

Where We Come From

CREATION MYTHS.
All cultures have creation stories which tell of the way they see
who they are, where they came from, why they are here and what
they feel is the purpose of their lives.

Here is a Creation Myth based on Native American teachings
……..

In the beginning was Great Grandmother Wakan
She is also called 'The Great Round'
Great Grandmother Wakan is the seed or egg of potential for all
creation
Great grandmother is the zero or circle which is all in potential
The first number of creation is the zero

'Before' creation,
'Every-thing' is the same as 'No-thing'
The zero is both no-thing and every-thing
The moment of creation is when Great Grandmother Wakan
Is joined by Great Grandfather Ssquan

Great Grandfather is like a Lightningbolt
Great Grandfather, the spark of light,

Penetrates Great Grandmother, the seed, the egg,
And they explode into a Universe of yin and yang,
Feminine and Masculine

Creation takes place

In this moment of creation, three dimensional existence begins

Consciousness has birthed itself –

Into a multitude of forms

Now it can experience life

Which is Itself in manifestation

....

Everything that exists is part of The-All
And exists within the Circle-of-The-All.

The Circle-of-the-All has no boundaries and there can be no-thing
outside the all

Humans have given 'The-All' many names

To the Native American people, it is often known as
'Wakantanka'

Wakan means 'holy' and Tanka means 'a lot'!

Many people use the term 'Great Spirit'

Others use these terms: - Creator, The Force, The Un-Nameable,
God, Allah, Aluna, The Great Tyrant, The Great Mystery....
Here is another creation story. This one I wrote as a simple way

of expressing the beginning of all things.

Once upon a No-Time in a No-Place existed Consciousness
Of Absolutely-Nothing
Absolutely-Nothing had lived in this No-Where place for Eternity
Which is a very very long No-Time
Especially as nothing always happened there
(Just like a television set with no programme... and no screen and
no box!)
After such a long boring no-time Absolutely-Nothing became
absolutely fed up!

And so it transpired that on one highly auspicious No-Day
(Had there been any days)
at the most auspicious No-Time of All (Had there been any time)
When all the planets were in perfect alignment (had there been
any planets)
Absolutely-Nothing did the only thing that No-Thing can do
to create Some-Thing
It split itself into TWO opposite energies
One part we call Yin, the primal FEMININE, the spiral vortex
And the other Yang, the primal MASCULINE, the wave of light
The Yin and the Yang were naturally attracted to each other
by their differences.....
But when they got close they found they were also repelled from
each other
by their differences....
So they began to dance, closer and further, closer and further,
around and around, closer and further, around and around....

Absolutely-Nothing was so pleased that So Much Something was
happening
That He/She/It began to laugh
And she laughed and laughed and laughed so hard
Until all of a sudden she burst –

In a **GREAT BIG BANG**..............

And became a UNIVERSE in SPACE and TIME

This book is about adventures of Consciousness on a small planet journeying around a small star on the edge of a rather minor galaxy somewhere on the outer reaches of that Universe......

THE STRUCTURE OF THE UNIVERSE

ENERGIES OF THE COSMOS

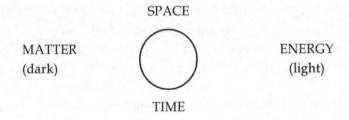

SPACE

MATTER   ENERGY
(dark)   (light)

TIME

From the Primordial explosion of Consciousness into Existence
came forth
the fire of Light, the Energy of Creation.
Light Energy sought to express its' Self and required
Time in which to do so.
Time needed space in which to move

Energy burst forth and in spreading out, some light spread
so widely that space appeared to be empty,
and some concentrated together in vortexes.

Concentrated vortexes of the Energy of Light are what we experience as Matter.

Everything is energy-waves (light) and energy-vortexes (matter). Thus everything is ultimately inter-changeable with everything else because it is ultimately the same energy.

Everything has a purpose and seeks to fulfill itself as efficiently and effectively as possible.

All things are born from the inner dark feminine yin vortex polarity.

All things come forth into the light of the outer masculine yang wave polarity.

The FOUR ELEMENTS
from which life (as we know it) is created

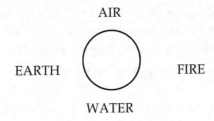

From the energy of Light comes Fire.
Fire expands bringing Wind.
Wind blows energy, condensing into gas.
From the mixing of elements comes Water.
From the spiralling of energy comes Matter.
The building blocks of the life we know are literally
fire , air, water and earth

Concentrations of fiery gas become stars and concentrations of cooled matter become planets. Consciousness thus comes to express itself as stars and planets. We can call them

STAR PEOPLE

and

PLANET PEOPLE

THE FOUR KINGDOMS OF MOTHER EARTH

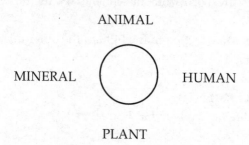

ANIMAL

MINERAL   HUMAN

PLANT

In the evolution of Consciousness on Mother Earth:-
The STONE PEOPLE came first. They experience time very slowly and changes take what may seem like an eternity to us. They hold the structure of the planet together, they are the rock upon which all is built. The stones are part of the mineral kingdom.

In the Stone People, Consciousness moves very slowly.

With the creation of water came the PLANT PEOPLE. To fulfill their existence they grow and sprout and seed, and when winter comes they fall back and die. New birth manifests again in the next spring season. The Tree People hold the surface soil of the earth together, and along with the plants they breath in carbon dioxide and breath out oxygen, thereby creating the atmosphere. The trees are the STANDING PEOPLE.

In the Plant People, Consciousness has evolved to express itself into life in a stationary manner. It grows, fruits, and dies in one place.

Through the creation of oxygen came air and the development of individual lungs as separate energy sources. From this came hearts and bellies and the development of the ANIMAL PEOPLE - the swimmers, crawlers, 4-leggeds and winged, who all have the gift of movement.

In the Animal People, Consciousness has gained vehicles in which it has the ability to transport itself, to mate and reproduce itself, to find food and shelter, and to fight if necessary for survival. Consciousness has moved further towards freedom and self-determination.

The HUMANS came last and have the gift of self-reflection. Humans are the beings who know 'I am' and who thus have the unique gift of conscious choice and the obligation of responsibility.

In the Human People, Consciousness has evolved to begin to know itself, to be able to consider its purpose in being alive and to make choices about its direction. Humans have the ability to think, imagine and create structures outside of themselves.

Many shamans teach that Great Spirit's Plan is that humans are Caretakers of the Earth and all her Kingdoms.

THE FOUR WORLDS OF MOTHER EARTH

WEST WORLD OF MOTHER EARTH - EARTH SPIRIT

Mother I feel you under my feet,
Mother I hear your heart beat

The Element of Earth
Form: Mountains, valleys, hills, plains, crags, tors, canyons,
Character: Solid, hard, material, weight, stable.

Mineral Kingdom
Form: Rocks, stones, crystals, boulders, sands, soil, compost, ores,
metals
Character: Holding, containment, structure, solidyfying,
stabilising, supporting

Earth my body

....

SOUTH WORLD OF MOTHER EARTH - WATER SPIRIT

Water spirits water spirits round my head
I'm so glad that I'm not dead!

The Element of Water

Form: Ocean, river, lake, stream, brook, rain, hail, snow, ice,
iceberg, pool, pond, waterfall, flood, cloud, mist, droplets, blood,
body fluids.
Character: Flowing, movement, purifying, quencher of thirst,
life through fluidity, exchanging of energies, cleanser

Plant Kingdom

Form: Trees, shrubs, herbs, vegetables, fruits, grasses, flowers,
cacti, medicinal plants, teacher-plants,
Character: Growing, giving, seeding, sprouting, providing,
replenishing, greening, transforming, multiplying, feeding,
Makers of oxygen, absorbers of CO_2

Water my blood

....

NORTH WORLD OF MOTHER EARTH - AIR SPIRIT

Fly like an eagle,
Fly so high,
Circle around the Universe
On wings of pure light

The Element of Air

Form: Wind, breeze, blow, gale, force, hurricane, tornado,
Character: Breath, carrier, communicator, mover, pusher,
provider of Manna.

Animal Kingdom

Form: Swimmers, creepers and crawlers, 4-leggeds, wingeds
Character: Receiving, giving, instinctual knowing, survival
skills, procreation.

Air My Breath

... ...

EAST WORLD OF MOTHER EARTH - FIRE SPIRIT

Fire, sacred fire, Burning through the night
Come to me in the dreamtime, Bring me visions of light
Circle round, spiral down, To these hearts open wide
Healing light burning bright, Dry these tears that I cry

The Element of Fire
Form: Fire, flame, flicker, glow, blaze, inferno, sun, star,
Character: Warmth, light, heat, glowing, transformation of
energy, alchemy, illumination.

Human Kingdom
Form: Black people, white people, red people, yellow people
Metis (mixed blood) people.
Character: Creating, making, thinking, compassion, love, hate,
fear, courage, beauty, bullshit, understanding, theoretising,
judgements, addictions, bravery, cowardice, selfishness,
selflessness, soul, spirit, violence, passion.

Fire my Spirit
....

THE FOUR HUMAN RACES OF MOTHER EARTH

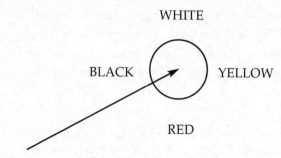

WHITE

BLACK   YELLOW

RED

CENTRE: RAINBOW PEOPLE – THOSE OF MIXED BLOOD.

The teaching is –

The Red People are placed in the South as they have the gift of understanding of the heart, of feeling, of all qualities associated with the element of water.

The Black People are placed in the West as their gift is of the body, of the physical realm, of the Earth element.

The White People are placed in the North as they have the gift of mind and of all things associated with the element of air.

The Yellow people are placed in the East as theirs is the gift of vision and all things associated with the element of fire.

The Rainbow (mixed blood) people are placed in the centre as they belong to all directions.

THE FOUR COLOURS

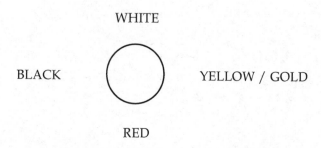

WHITE

BLACK   YELLOW / GOLD

RED

The yellow / gold of the East is the colour of the sun, our Sky Father, around whom we travel and who gives us light, heat, and a multitude of other rays. We are part of the Sun as our Mother the Earth is part of the Sun. We are children of the solar system, which is a child of the Galaxy, which is a child of this dimension of the Cosmos, which is a child of All-Creation or God.

The red of the South is the red of summer, of blood, of the heart. The South is the place of emotion or energy-motion, it is the 'Close-To' place where the forces of 'I-me and mine' are clamouring to be understood and embraced.

The black of the West is the colour of the Within. It is the dark of the Inner World, of the womb where all new creation gestates. Black is the absence of light. We need both light and absence of light-one cannot exist without the other, and only when both are in balance are we able to see and discriminate.

The white of the North is the colour of age and maturity, of the snows of winter, of the clarity of all colours together. It is the place of the giveaway, of living for others, of service, when age and experience have brought wisdom. That is the direction we are intended to follow and that evolution seeks to take us.

THE FOUR SEASONS

WINTER

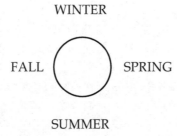

FALL   SPRING

SUMMER

SPRING is placed in the East with the rising sun
SUMMER is placed in the South when the sun is at its height
(northern hemisphere)
AUTUMN is in the West of the setting sun
as the night draws longer

WINTER is the North, where comes the cold, the snow and
the ice

FOUR FOLDEDNESS.

Our everyday world is based on the number four and by looking
at the following examples we can see how this is. In the Medicine
Wheel teachings this is expressed as The Four Directions.

THE FOUR DIVISIONS OF SPACE
LENGTH, BREADTH, VOLUME, TIME

THE FOUR BASIC GEOMETRIC FIGURES.
LINE, SQUARE, CIRCLE, TRIANGLE
THE FOUR ASPECTS OF ARITHMETIC
ADDITION, SUBTRACTION, MULTIPLICATION, DIVISION

THE FOUR ELEMENTS BASIC TO ALL ORGANIC SUBSTANCE
ARE HYDROGEN (fire), NITROGEN (air), OXYGEN (water)
AND CARBON (earth).

THE FOUR UNIVERSAL FORCE FIELDS ARE
ELECTROMAGNETISM, GRAVITY, STRONG NUCLEAR AND
WEAK NUCLEAR

THE FOUR QUALITIES OF ATMOSPHERE
WARM, COLD, MOIST, DRY

THE FOUR TYPES OF ROCKS IN THE BODY OF THE EARTH
ARE IGNEOUS, SEDIMENTARY, CONGLOMERATE AND
METAMORPHIC

THE FOUR TYPES OF TISSUE THAT MAKE UP THE BODY
ARE NERVE, BONE, BLOOD AND FLESH

THE FOUR COMPONENTS OF THE DNA ARE KNOWN AS
THYMINE(T), CYTOSINE(C), ADENINE(A), GUANINE(G)

And so on!

IN CONCLUSION -

The structure of the Spirit World is THREE - THE TRINITY

1   ALL-THAT -IS
2   ALL-THAT-IS FEMININE
3   ALL-THAT-IS MASCULINE

and the structure of the Manifest World is FOUR
THREE + FOUR = SEVEN.

SEVEN IS THE NUMBER OF THE CREATOR
MANIFESTED INTO CREATION –

Hence: 'Seven Days' of Creation.

SEVEN IS   –-

THE 'DREAM' OF CREATOR

LET US NOW EXAMINE CREATOR'S DREAM.......

SECTION ONE

PART 1: THE FOUR DIRECTIONS

We co-habit this planet with all our brother and sister humans and all the other kingdoms. We have our unique place in the scheme of things and there are many forces which work upon us, none less than the limitations of the human body–our 'Vehicle-Of-Experience' or 'Earth-Lodge'. The Medicine Wheel teachings illuminate our situation and shed light on our lives. Anything can be placed on the Medicine Wheel, and when its rightful place is found, the power that it exerts and the powers surrounding it reveal much about it and about our relationship to it.

OUR FOUR ASPECTS

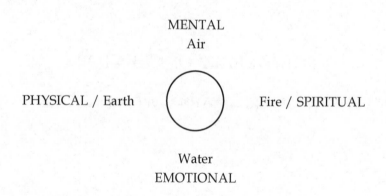

MENTAL
Air

PHYSICAL / Earth   Fire / SPIRITUAL

Water
EMOTIONAL

LIGHT AND DARK.

It is very important to understand that light and dark are equally important. As are day and night, sun and earth, feminine and masculine, inner and outer, and so on. All opposite forces are equally necessary because our lives exist between the two polarities.

Dark is often thought of as bad while light is espoused as good. But you cannot see in all-light any more than you can in all-dark.

We only see when both are present.

Life is lived in shadow and it is the parts of the shadow where we don't see clearly that problems lie. This is what we will stalk throughout this book - the bringing of that which is unconscious into consciousness.

THE FOUR ASPECTS

We humans are four-aspect beings. We are matter; our physical body is 'walking earth', our bones are the stones, our flesh is the soil, our blood is the water and our breath is the air. Our bodies are created by the Earth and the Sun. We are the Earth and the Sun seeing themselves through their self-reflective creation, the human being.

We are emotion - feeling. We have needs, wants and desires. Our spirit-essence takes on an earth-lodge, a physical body, to experience emotion – energy-motion. Some have suggested that Spirit cannot do this anywhere else in the Universe and that Planet Earth therefore gives a unique gift to evolution.

E-motion is a gift of physical life on Mother Earth. Emotion is connected to the element of water, which is our blood and a surprisingly large percentage of our physical vehicle.

We are mind - we think, calculate, extrapolate and invent. We also judge, criticize and limit. We create our own experience of reality through our thoughts and our emotions.

We are Spirit - we come from the Spirit World into body to experience life in the limitation of third dimensional gross matter. Here we experience our-self as if we are a self-directed individual. At all times we have the choice to align our individual will with the Will of Great-Spirit-Creator - or not to.

We die to spirit to enter matter and we will die to matter to re-enter spirit. Nothing is lost, everything is changed. Our life experience is added to the collective of all experience. We are aspects of the Great Spirit, God, Creator, The-Everything, which is experiencing itself and growing in wisdom and knowledge as a result.

As above, so below. As we grow and develop, so does The-

Everything.

At the end of our earth-life we will die to this realm and be reborn back in our true home, the world of Spirit.

. . .

Our four aspects relate to THE FOUR TIMES

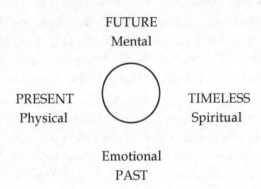

FUTURE
Mental

PRESENT   TIMELESS
Physical   Spiritual

Emotional
PAST

Our emotions relate to the past. We feel in the present time but the memories and associations which colour our feelings are all from our past. Perhaps, to clarify, let us look at the emotion of fear. There are basically two kinds of fear. There is real time physical fear, necessary for safety, the kind that happens in an earthquake or if one is standing in the path of a large approaching vehicle. The automatic flight / fight system takes over and we act without inhibition or the slightest concern about what someone might think of us.

Then there is all the other fear, emotional fear, anxiety, worry, concern. Early in an experiential workshop I often pass a talking stick around the circle asking participants to introduce themselves. One can frequently 'see' anxiety preceding the stick by about four or five places! This fear is emotional and from the past, from our personal history, and it is a consequence of accumulated lack of self-esteem, self-worth and confidence. It is an 'enemy' which can be faced, worked through and conquered, with immensely beneficial consequences for the quality of life.

Our mind tends to fixate on the future. That is part of its job–to lay out plans for the future. But when it won't stop and is permanently out there struggling with what might be, what might happen, what problem might occur, we become neurotic and anxious–it feeds our negative emotions and keeps us away from being fully conscious here and now. The mind is a good servant but a bad master.

Our body is always in the present. The physical only exists in the present moment; there is no other moment for the body. As a child we spent lots of time in the present, playing and getting so absorbed that time seemed to disappear. The play played the child - and once upon a time, that was you and me.

When time disappears, we are through the magical gateway into the timeless realm of the 'East'. Here we can be moved by the spirit and touched by the magic.

'HAPPINESS IS SOMETHING YOU KNOW YOU JUST HAD'.

It is when we are in the state of just-being rather than the state of trying and doing that true deep happiness and joy occurs. But we only know it has occurred when we return to the doing state - and then we are not in the being state any more!

Now let us look further into our four aspects. We humans have four experiences of self. We Can Call Them ......

THE FOUR 'SHIELDS'

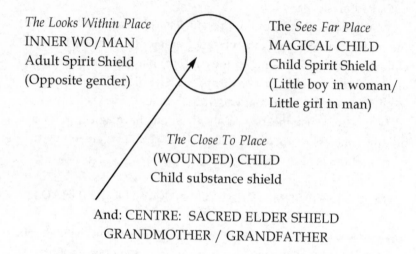

The knowing place
EVERYDAY ADULT
Adult substance shield

The Looks Within Place
INNER WO/MAN
Adult Spirit Shield
(Opposite gender)

The *Sees Far Place*
MAGICAL CHILD
Child Spirit Shield
(Little boy in woman/
Little girl in man)

The Close To Place
(WOUNDED) CHILD
Child substance shield

And: CENTRE: SACRED ELDER SHIELD
GRANDMOTHER / GRANDFATHER

A 'shield' in this sense is not something used as protection but more as a declaration, like a Coat of Arms, but rather than a static one this is open to change. For example, outside a traditional Native American tipi one might see a circular painting depicting scenes. Often this might be a medicine painting, a shield of one of the occupants which graphically depicts the person's inner world.

NORTH SHIELD

The adult north part of us is the thinker who runs our ordinary life for us and keeps our future plans in order. It is the 'shield' or 'essence' of our adult physical being. This is our everyday functioning adult persona through which we live in the ordinary world. The primary task of this part of our-self is to guide us through the day-to-day trials and tests of life and to see that we survive and thrive.

The North Shield is our shield of common sense and 'knowing', which we have when we are in tune with our primal instincts and have not been 'educated' out of them. The allies of the North are wisdom, knowledge, balance, harmony, alignment - all those abilities which are natural to an animal living in its natural habitat. The enemy of the North shield is 'clarity' - which can seem confusing at first. Clarity is an ally when we see something clearly for the first time but beware how quickly it can turn into dogma! What the term really means here is most easily understood by the commonplace term - 'bullshit'. While wisdom is the real thing which we can touch deep within, bullshit is the mockery of wisdom, the impersonator, which we have to make do with when our natural knowing is inhibited and we merely regurgitate other people's theories and dogmas. It is all that we have left if we sell out our True Self to belong and to be approved and accepted and hold only the same thoughts and opinions as everybody else, the consensus agreement of how things are.

SOUTH SHIELD

The shield of the South is the inner child, sometimes called the 'wounded child', and is the emotional aspect of us. It is the part of us that gets angry, loving, fearful, excited, sad, joyful, jealous, happy–that runs the gamut of emotions. When the child within holds wounds of the past, our emotional responses are often an inaccurate response to the actual stimulus received in the present, and thus they can create more painful situations to deal with. It is the healing of this part of us that comes first on the Great Journey of the Spiritual Warrior.

The South Shield contains the history of our childhood. During the process of growing up, of education and socialisation, we tend lose much of the natural childlike state of trust and innocence. Most come to live with fear, inhibition, shyness, doubt of self-worth and the right to be and express who they truly are. Some remain hooked onto parents, either following their ways, or else living in negative reaction to them, still seeking their approval and/or disapproval.

The loss of puberty rites in western culture has very serious ramifications in how we live our lives. It has left many adults living partially out of their child shield instead of becoming mature adults able to take full responsibility for themselves. In growing up it is natural that a child experiences betrayal and abandonment. This is coded into fairy stories. In the old cultures which maintained their natural understanding of the psyche, it was acted out ritually, and thus the trauma was acknowledged publicly and made understandable and acceptable.

To become an adult, a child has to learn that parents are not the gods that they appeared to be in babyhood. The first god we meet on our life journey is Mother. She is literally Mother-God to us in babyhood as our survival depends upon her. We feed at her breast, unless she had a physical problem that prevented her or she was filled up with unnatural dogma such as the idea that bottle feeding is better. The second 'god' we meet is Father-God, our physical father, unless nature has been interfered with and he is not there or is not equipped to play his proper role.

A natural time comes when the child has to start making his/her own decisions. The child reaches a stage of challenging the parents and finding out they are not infallible. What follows is uncertainty, a falling out of the childhood 'Garden of Eden' - the place of simple instinctual unquestioning trusting and the beginning of taking responsibility for Self. If this happens naturally and easily, all progresses well. If it happens suddenly without preparation and without guidance, a trauma occurs and the child can get stuck and experience soul loss through abandonment. A degree of abandonment, however, is a natural and necessary growth point around the time of puberty. In the old puberty rituals the young were taken away and put through trials and tests after which they came back to the village with a new name and status in the community. In this way what would potentially create a trauma of uncertainty is resolved through public acknowledgement of the whole tribe or village.

WEST SHIELD
The West shield is the Adult Spirit Shield and is the Inner-Adult

Spirit-Being who can be felt as the opposite polarity to the everyday adult self. Man's inner woman, woman's inner man. It is the inner part of us that we touch through spiritual work or deep states of connectedness. By touching this part frequently and getting to spend more and more of our life connected to the Inner Self, we deepen our experience of life and get to live with greater resources, more colour, and much more ability to deal with life's challenges and tests. We also gain a much different perspective on the purpose of being alive. The seeming importance of the struggle for more of this, that or the other goes into the background, and qualities of relationship, friendship, connection with people, the earth, animals, trees, the planet, the spirit and existence, take on a greater importance.

EAST SHIELD

The East shield is the magical child aspect of us, the part of us that knows how to play, that is timeless and beyond the confines of physical reality. This is the part of us who is boundless and who does not know anxiety, fear, inhibition, limits; the part of us who just glories in existence.

This is the child aspect of us that has no past or future, has never been hurt, traumatised, conditioned or 'educated'. It is the magical-free-child part of our-self that we experience when we get fully into laughter, spontaneity, play, dance and purposeless being. The magical child is manifest within us when we are so involved with what we are doing that we lose any sense of time. It is the sun, the divine light within, the inspiration - in-spirit - timeless beingness that is us when we have no concern with past or future, no hidden agendas, no 'trying', no effort to be 'something' or 'someone'. It is the place of just-being without a single self-conscious thought. The dance is dancing the dancer. This child is the child of the cosmos, of the Great Mother and Great Father.

CENTRE: SACRED ELDER SHIELD.
GRANDMOTHER / GRANDFATHER

There are Four Directions, but there is always the Centre also, the fifth direction without which the others could not be.

This is the place of the Old One who is truly the Wise Elder and guide for the young and the busy. We all come to old age, and old age nowadays usually means being shoved away, out of it, rejected, into a home or hospital.

In the way of the Ancients, old age was a time when one had accumulated the wisdom and knowledge of years of human life and thus had much to give. To truly be a Wise Elder, one has to have walked a path of self-development and gained deep self-knowledge so that one becomes wise and knowledgeable on matters of life and spirit, of loving, caring and nurturing, and a strong, resourceful person who 'Walks Their Talk' and 'Touches The World With Beauty'. One must have developed understanding of the ways of the Cosmos through working with nature, both external and internal, and a deep knowledge of the ways of human beings. Both inner and outer understanding and connection come together to make a power-full person of knowledge and wisdom.

HEALING THE DIVIDED SELF - MARRYING THE SHIELDS.

A way of seeing the healing of the self is as a 'marrying' of the Child of the South, with its fears and its wounds, with the Child of the East who is always whole. The Child of the East can melt away the wounds and pains of the South Child.

Simultaneously one seeks to marry the Adult of the North, with all his anxious planning and concerns for future and, with the Adult Spirit Being of the West who lives fully in the present.

This is the Sacred Marriage of the Prince and Princess, familiar in so many fairy stories. It is the marriage of the Outer and Inner of One's-Self into a truly autonomous, self responsible, self actualising being.

Hence we erase the effects of our personal history and become whole and mature, living fully in the Here and Now, with no hidden agendas or secrets.

Oh if it were only so easy!

FOUR STAGES OF HUMAN DEVELOPMENT.

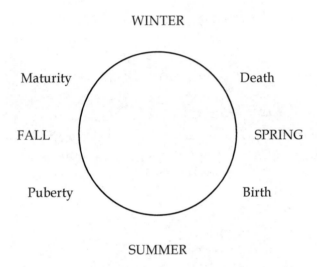

The four stages - or seasons – of human growth and development correspond to the four seasons of the Earth

CHILDHOOD - Summer - The instinctive, emotional, physical, outward looking, reactive, immediate, needing, playful, innocent, sensation seeking, irrational soul of the child

ADOLESCENCE - Fall - The self-conscious, inward looking, questioning, psychological soul of the developing adolescent. The Fall - from the innocence of childhood into the experience of self-consciousness, and the awareness of time and death.

MATURITY - Winter - The rational, responsible, self-controlled, interdependent mind of the mature adult. Work, parenthood, sharing, providing, community. Attainment of enough wisdom to help the community to survive through the cold of winter.

ELDERSHIP / NEWBORN - DEATH AND BIRTH - Spring - The

wise spiritual elder who is withdrawing from the everyday as the journey ends; the spirit of the newborn who is entering life's new journey. The end and the beginning.

CHOREOGRAPHY OF ENERGY.

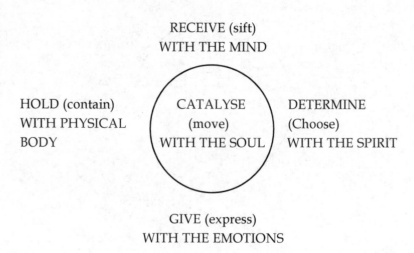

RECEIVE (sift)
WITH THE MIND

HOLD (contain)   CATALYSE   DETERMINE
WITH PHYSICAL   (move)   (Choose)
BODY   WITH THE SOUL   WITH THE SPIRIT

GIVE (express)
WITH THE EMOTIONS

How do you use your energy? Let me put that another way – what do you do with your emotions, with your feelings? When you were a child, you no doubt expressed them freely, as pretty much we all did. But by the time we get to adulthood most of us have learned to hold many of our emotions in. This is necessary for much everyday interaction, but when taken to extreme and when no outlet is found, emotions get stuck inside with disastrous consequences for our physical and emotional wellbeing.

It is healthy to 'give' with emotions (South of the Wheel), speaking them, sharing them, expressing them; whilst holding, 'containing' with the physical body (West). When that gets reversed and we hold the emotions in, we often tend to 'give' with the physical body, perhaps in a flare of temper or in hitting out in some inappropriate way. Alternatively we may hold our emotions in and not express them, and if we do that over a long period of time, we are likely to get undesirable physical symptoms and illness. This is also when we tend to become accident prone as our

stulti'
awf
e'

ɔhow to find a way of expression. An
ɔaused when people are unable to
ɔds to go somewhere and if
ʿt bursts forth destruc-

ρ are the North and the
the mind, North, is for
information. It is not for
ʿe up your mind' is a virtual
making are placed in the East
ʿe of Spirit. The lesson is this: sort
ʿieving a sense of clarity – and then
ʿation at your finger tips, invite the

deci.   ʿ, from your Essense.

Then ι.   ʿ way around the wheel, the South and
the East can gʿ   up or perhaps more accurately misused.
This is the misuse oι ʿ ʿe two 'child' energies. The South is the place
of the 'wounded' child that carries all our experience of past
emotional life, while the East is the place of the 'magical' child
which carries nothing at all - it has no past and no future as it is the
experience of timelessness. It is easy - and seductive - when
confronted with difficult emotional issues to 'convert' them to
'spiritual' matters and rationalise all sorts of behaviour as 'what
spirit has told me to do' or 'I am so deeply spiritual that you (lesser
mortal) wouldn't understand'. This is a trap that 'deeply spiritual'
or 'religious' people can fall into and sooner or later they tend to
land up in a state of depression because that is one of the
Universe's ways of forcing us to confront things - and life pushes
us all to confront our emotions and work to understand what they
are telling us. There is no way life will let us off this task.

The North and the West are the two adult parts of us, the
everyday rational adult and the inner spirit adult. Here we need to
run everyday life from our North shield - and rationality will serve
us well - while running our inner life from our West shield. If we
reverse these polarities, we will get massive failure trying to use
rationality to work with spirit and introspection to run the

everyday!

Summing this up another way:-

Balanced choreography of energy means, firstly, to keep the West and the South in good balance. Use the physical body to hold and contain your energy while with your emotions you give, communicate, reveal how you feel, express your passions, desires and needs.

Secondly it means to keep the North and East in harmony so that the mind is used to receive and sift information, to calculate and think through, while the decisions are put to Spirit. This rewrites the saying 'Make up your mind' to 'Never make up your mind ever again but let yourself be guided by Spirit'.

When these forces are in harmony all is well, but when they get out of balance, which is only too 'normal' today unfortunately, the result is unhappiness and confusion.

HUMAN CHOREOGRAPHY IN BEAUTY

RECEIVING with compassion and caring

HOLDING a space,
Holding another
with intimacy

OPENNESS
Heart to heart
soul to soul

DETERMINATION,
CHOICE, with love
and passion

GIVING with gentleness

GIVE gently by creating a heart space when gathering together with others.

HOLD with intimacy by caring for another's physical space and body.

RECEIVE with compassion by treating others with respect, honour and dignity.

DETERMINE, make choices, with love and passion by keeping in touch with spiritual vision and purpose.

Be open SOUL TO SOUL with another so that one is in tune with another's life purpose.

THE FOUR PRIMARY HUMAN EMOTIONS

Here is way of putting the primary emotions onto the medicine wheel.

THE SHADOW OR NEGATIVE EMOTIONS

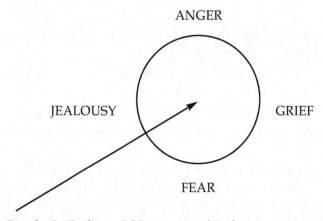

ANGER

JEALOUSY   GRIEF

FEAR

Results In Feelings Of Separation / Isolation

AND THE BEAUTY EMOTIONS

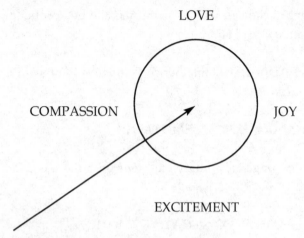

LOVE

COMPASSION   JOY

EXCITEMENT

Results In Feelings Of Unity / Oneness

Out of a mind-set of separation and isolation comes the unhappy emotions of fear, anger, grief, and jealousy

Out of the mind-set of unity and oneness comes the happy emotions of excitement, love, joy and compassion.

The root is how we see and feel ourselves to be in the world, and that comes from the description of the world we tell ourselves to believe in.

When we approach from unity and oneness, knowing ourselves to be in a world that is divine, we live in a beautiful connected world. In this world we are natural ecologists, we make love not war, we support and share rather than compete, we know there is abundance (so long as we are awake to it), in the sense of there being simply 'enough', and we know that other is another aspect of 'self' so respect for other beings is natural.

When we see ourselves living in a separated world with a separated god who is somewhere else - and most likely sitting in judgment of us - we can easily feel that the earth is against us and that we have to own bits of it and manipulate its nature for our benefit. We fear others are against us and will try to take the little that is ours so we need boundaries around us and armies and war, we feel we must compete and prove our-self the best or at least adequate, so we live in fear, protecting ourselves from enemies we think are out to get us.

Which of those feels 'normal'?

> It all comes down to how we look at the world,
> How we frame our world,
> How we see our relationship to the cosmos,
> The story we tell ourselves of how it is.
> Consider this — -

CULTURAL MYTHOLOGIES AND 'GOD'.

A culture lives by the stories that the people tell themselves of how it is and what is right and what is normal. These stories are so deeply held that they are largely unconscious and invisible and they are considered by the majority to be way beyond question. For example, consider the myth that man was thrown out of the 'Garden of Eden' and is therefore a fallen and fundamentally flawed being in need of redemption, forgiveness and a 'saviour' to save him from himself. What an extraordinary idea! Our ancestors way back, from whom the teachings in this book have come, held no such nonsensical beliefs. They understood how things are by studying the natural world and they considered themselves to be a part of this world and of Creation, not separate from it and not superior or inferior to it.

But then during the time range of around 6 – 10,000 years ago, agriculture began as people found they could cultivate land, bringing about a gradual but immense revolution. Not just a change from nomadic hunter-gatherers to settled villages but a change in the concept of and relationship to creator-creation. A 'god' was invented who said that 'He' had given man dominion over everything and that the whole development of the earth and all her kingdoms had been just so man could appear and take over. No longer was man a part of the world, he was the boss and the whole crowning glory of creation! But that meant he was also separate and alone and therefore needed to be competitive to prove his individual worth. I remember the cultural mores of the traditional style boarding school I attended, which were that a boy had no value as himself, his value was purely in what he could win - for the glory of the school, his house (i.e. small unit within the school) and lastly himself.

It is interesting that this change is coded into the story of Cain and Abel in the Bible. Cain the tiller of the soil kills Abel the hunter-gatherer-herder. i.e. The coming of agriculture kills the way of the hunter-gatherer. Then 'God' banishes Cain from the 'Garden' and tells him he and his descendents will only live by the sweat of their brows. i.e. The nomadic lifestyle was one of relative ease but agriculture is seriously hard work. Many indigenous cultures whose way of life has not been ruined by 'developed' nations actually live a life of greater ease than we do and are still in the 'garden' where 'god', i.e. nature, provides on a regular basis. We might consider their lifestyle 'poor' but it is ours that is full of stress, doubt, anxiety, competition, lack of self-esteem, drug taking, depression, mental illness, heart attacks and so on.

This 'god' was said to have written a whole big book (compliantly compiled by his earthly servants) to 'prove' that 'he' was in charge and was to be worshipped. For this worship to be instilled in the human race it was important to persuade them that they were worthless, fallen and flawed, and hence the bible begins with an appropriate myth. This myth also conveniently disenfranchises women (who might not have bought into the nonsense so readily) by making out they are an inferior species who were only created as an afterthought by this 'god' for the sole benefit of men. These extraordinary contrary-to-nature concepts are still held by many otherwise intelligent people of the twenty first century to be 'the truth'!

It is important to realise that since that time, things have gone badly wrong. So badly wrong that the human race is facing a serious possibility of a partial extinction that may well take many other species with it. Many species are already extinct through ignorant actions of the human race and the earth-changes-pollution-degradation that have happened already. The collective cultural mythologies of growth, development, control, more, better, increase GDP, make higher profit, consume ever more 'things', are just not working. They are creating a mega crisis for our home planet and everything and everyone upon her. And we, collectively, are not listening, or at least only a relative few of us. We are steaming headlong into a crisis that is coming about because we have adopted a flawed cultural myth and a deeply flawed 'god'.

THE FOUR EXPRESSIONS OF POWER

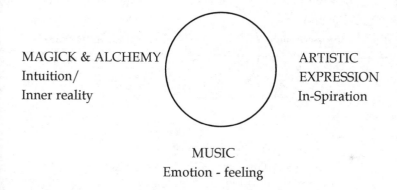

MATHEMATICS, SCIENCE, TECHNOLOGY
Thinking

MAGICK & ALCHEMY
Intuition/
Inner reality

ARTISTIC
EXPRESSION
In-Spiration

MUSIC
Emotion - feeling

Mental knowledge, logic and wisdom, are expressed as science, mathematics, geometry, algebra, numbers, quantities, the quantification of relationship, the study of how the Universe works which is the study of the 'Mind of God'. Technology is the ability to create change in the external world.

Magick and alchemy are the application of the same study to the inner landscape - the study of how the subtle, non-physical Universe works.

Artistic expression is our attempt to express our illumination, our 'seeing', our insight, and to convey it so others can see, feel, hear, sense, taste, intuit, and grasp it too.

Music is our expression of trust and innocence through the

medium of sound.

Prana, the Breath Of Life, the pure Life Force Energy is the root of all life, all power, all expression, all activity, all existence in this dimension.

THE FOUR GODDESSES OF THE DIRECTIONS
(From Native American Mythology)

RATTLING HAIL WOMAN
Teaches us to be concerned for the welfare of all beings
And to giveaway for the good of all

CHANGING WOMAN
Teaches the rhythm of
continual ebb and flow
and of the inter-connect-
edness of all living
things and of our
responsibility to our
mother the earth

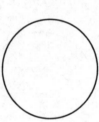

SPIDER WOMAN
Creates and re- creates
the Universe
reminding us that the
weaver and the web
are One

WHITE BUFFALO WOMAN
Brings the medicine pipe to the people
to remind us of the sacredness of all things

South is the place of White Buffalo Woman who brings the Medicine Pipe to the people to teach and remind us of the sacredness of all things. The South is where we experience the warrior's first enemy, fear, and learn to do battle and not be overcome. The animal totems of the South are Little Mouse who reminds that the big picture is made up of lots of little details, Coyote who tricks us into all sorts of scrapes in which we learn and grow, and Serpent who sheds his skin and teaches that we too must shed our past to move on and to grow.

West is the place of Changing Woman who teaches of constantly flowing and moving cycles, of the continual rhythm of ebb and flow, and of the interconnectedness of all that exists and our responsibility to nurture life and all living things. The West reminds us of our responsibility to our Mother, the Earth, who gives us the incredible gift of life and who meets all our needs constantly. The animal totem is Bear who hibernates through the winter and reminds us to look deep within for the source of our truth. West is the place of the wise women who hold communities and families together.

The North is the place of Rattling Hail Woman who holds the Universe in her hands and teaches that we must be involved in the welfare of all beings.

We learn that we are part of a collective and that our individuality is completely interwoven and inter-dependent with that of our group, our country, all humans, all kingdoms, the Planet herself. This is the time of spiritual maturity as we come to understand that our wisdom, knowledge and experience are to be shared for the good of all - for the survival and thriving of all. The animal totems are buffalo who gives all of himself so the people may live, wolf who is pathfinder, teacher and keeper of the family.

East is the domain of Spider Woman who weaves her web, continually creating and re-creating the Universe, reminding us that the Weaver and the Web are One. It is the place of mens' council and of the heyeokah, the contrary-joker-comedian who teaches truth through showing the world upside down. The animal totem is eagle who flies high and connects us to the upper realms of the spirit world.

A HUMAN BEING'S BASIC NEEDS

We all of us have basic needs and these are 'needs' not 'wants'. If we don't have these, we don't survive. We need adequate food and clean water, adequate shelter and clothing, adequate sleep and dreaming. Experiments have been done in sleep deprivation that have shown that without REM dreaming sleep, we lose our ability to function. This is the internal filing system dealing with the day's experiences.

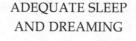

ADEQUATE SLEEP
AND DREAMING

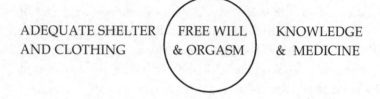

ADEQUATE SHELTER   FREE WILL   KNOWLEDGE
AND CLOTHING   & ORGASM   & MEDICINE

ADEQUATE FOOD
AND WATER

We also need adequate 'knowledge' and 'medicine'. Without mind-food we lose our sense of direction, our ability to see a way forward. This is what I experienced in my mid-life crisis and from which I did not recover until I found new and meaningful 'mind-food'. In addition we need adequate free will and orgasm. The Wheel teaches that orgasm goes with free will, which is our ability to make our own decisions and determine our own life.

This may seem a controversial idea but look at it this way. Our sexuality is the most basic creative part of ourselves. Through sex we create new life, only through sex is our race continued. Sexual power is both the primal energy of sexuality and also our creative energy, our individuality, our very Self which seeks expression and fulfillment through physical life. It is our sex that leads us on many a merry dance, that pushes us out to meet and unite with others, that creates the mixing of peoples - and the existence of new ones! Sex is probably the single greatest stimulator and mover within each of us. If that natural power is frustrated, controlled, repressed, limited, rejected, made in some way shameful, then a part of our soul dies and we become disempowered, we lose a part of our self - and therefore we become more easily controllable by those who would seek power over us. If we shut off natural easy expression of our sexuality we kill some of our vitality and our spirit – and bang goes a chunk of our free will and our ability to determine our own life journey.

PART 2: THE WARRIOR'S JOURNEY

BECOMING A SPIRITUAL WARRIOR

LIVING AUTHENTICALLY
and autonomously

FREEDOM
from physical
slavery and
oppression

SEEKING THE
MYSTERY
Mastering the
automatic-self

FREE WILL to make
our own conscious
choice

FOLLOWING YOUR BLISS
- acting on your heart's desire

In many traditions, a person who consciously steps on the path of personal transformation is known as a **Spiritual Warrior**.

Here are a few words from Hyemeyohsts Storm quoting his teacher Estcheemah in his book *Lightningbolt* pp359.

"Realise once and for all time, that what other people think of you does not matter. Only what you think of yourselves matters. All these other people are of no consequence. Remember that most humans can easily be impressed and easily flattered into believing anything.

Don't flatter yourselves. Don't be so crude and mundane as to believe that you matter to the world. Until the second you become valuable to your Self, you are meaningless, and your life is meaningless. You must work hard to understand and care for yourself. When you do this, then you will be able to have meaning in your Life"

The task of a Spiritual Warrior is to do battle with the enemies within. To battle with such familiar enemies as, for example, lazyness, self-pity, emotional needyness, self-criticism, lack of feelings of worth, dependency on others' approval, the seduction of glamour and celebrity, shame, blame of others and oneself, denial or avoidance of difficult truths, guilt, and so on.

The Warrior's task is to build her Self into a being who knows self-worth and how to self-care and who 'Walks-In-Beauty' on the earth. For many of us this is a virtual revolution in thinking, a re-creation of our self. To live with this attitude and awareness one needs no self aggrandizement props, no emotional defences, no dependencies, no needyness, no expectations and no shyness or inhibition.....

Just think of the energy released by _Not-Doing_ all that!

South – the emotional realm. A heartfelt desire to become a master of life and leave behind the slave-like existence of dependency on how others see you for self-approval.

North – the mental realm. A desire for the authenticity of being and living as yourself and not according to whether others recognise you or not. A sense of true autonomy in and over life.

West – the physical realm. A sense of freedom to live your own life, to choose where you live, to choose your work, and to be the creator of your life within the limits of being human.

East – the spiritual realm. To gain a real sense of freewill in living your life as co-creator with Great Spirit, Creator of All Existence.

Centre. Exploration into the mystery of self – and therefore the mystery of Existence (God). Mastery of yourself so that you are no longer at the effect of your emotions and your past, but are manifestor of your own future and co-creator of your own destiny.

When we truly start to look at how much we 'free' people, people of the 'free world' (to say nothing of those unfortunate enough to live in overtly repressive dictatorships), are actually subtly controlled and restricted, we can get a shock to the core. When we look at what actually gets into the media versus what is hidden from our knowledge; what kind of 'consciousness' is commonly promoted as normal - money, greed, glamour, one-upmanship, instant gratification, seeking of celebrity etc; how money and physical objects are promoted as 'wealth', how religion is promoted to 'save' us by relieving us of the need to think, learn, experience, study, know or grow; one gets to see how we can be like 'passengers' on a ship who are constantly being blinded to the real nature of our voyage.

The warrior's task is to WAKE UP! The voyage is happening. When we were children we were at the mercy of all sorts of forces outside of our control, and it was natural and comforting to believe in a Father-Christmas-Big-Daddy figure. But as adults who have made the decision to walk consciously on a Spiritual Path of Personal Development, we have taken a conscious vow to awaken. This means giving up the false security of 'Father-Christmas-for-Adults', the imposter-god of fear who sits in judgment, and recognizing that we are part of the real Creator and are co-creators and co-responsible.

REQUIREMENTS TO BE A SPIRITUAL WARRIOR

WILLINGNESS TO SEEK REAL KNOWLEDGE FOR YOURSELF
And not slavishly follow common beliefs and dogmas

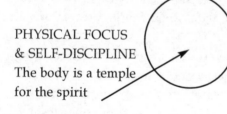

PHYSICAL FOCUS
& SELF-DISCIPLINE
The body is a temple
for the spirit

SPIRITUAL INTENT
Deep desire to explore
multi-dimensional reality

FOCUSED INTENT
TO AWAKEN

Emotional discipline -
HEARTFELT DESIRE
TO SUCCEED regardless of obstacles

Intent is the governor of the Universe. Intent is what makes things

happen, intent is what makes change, and change is what happens!
Without change, nothing happens. Intent preceeds change. We
humans are bundles of intent. We are walking intention. In a sense,
that is all we are - energy in the human form in third dimensional
reality intending.... All our waking hours are spent intending and
our dreaming hours are spent either resting the vehicle or
dreaming our next intent!

Another word for INTENT is PRAYER.

Prayer tends to be thought of as something one does formally,
perhaps repeating religious dogma. But actually, prayer is what
we do everytime we wish or we curse (which is also a wish!), so it
is something we do almost continuously. When we focus our
intention, we are praying effectively. When we want something,
wish we had more of something, or we damn and curse something
or someone, we are praying in an unfocused fashion, but our
intention is still going out into the world of energy. When we
want/want more, we are actually affirming lack.

   We live in the four dimensional Universe which is the Creator's
Intent to express It's Self through the existence of All Beings and
All-That-Is in this manifest realm. Everything changes all the time
in the Creator's Great Movement towards Evolution - The Creative
Intention.

   When our intent comes from our SPIRIT ESSENSE (or we can say
from our Inner Being) and when it is for the highest good of all
rather than the glory of little ego, it is likely to be a 'WARRIOR'S
INTENT'. The HEART'S DESIRE for this intent aids in the manifestation by engaging the feelings (emotion = energy-motion) towards
that which is desired. MENTAL KNOWLEDGE brings clarity and
focus to manifest the intention. Then, when PHYSICAL FOCUS
AND SELF-DISCIPLINE are applied towards the REAL-ISATION
OF THE INTENT, you are most likely to create what you desire.

   To add to the effectiveness of your intent - your prayer - SEE IT
AS DONE - see it ALREADY MANIFESTED in the realm of image
- I-the-MAGE, I-the-MAGICIAN, the MAGICAL REALM of I-

MAGE-A-NATION.

GIVE THANKS to Spirit for answering your prayer, do all that you need to in this dimension to aid and prepare for the coming change, and then simply wait with patience and with no concern for the manifestation to occur!

WHEEL OF TOOLS
to help and guide us on the journey:-

COUNCIL
MEDICINE WHEEL TEACHINGS
SHAMANIC JOURNEYS / SOUL RETRIEVAL
MEDITATION

CEREMONY	MOTHER	VISION QUEST
DANCE &	NATURE	PLAY (Purposeless
MOVEMENT	FATHER	creativity)
EARTH AWARENESS	SUN	

DOCTORING THE SOUL
(PSYCHOTHERAPY/HYPNOTHERAPY ETC.)
STUDY OF PERSONAL MYTHOLOGY
(The stories we tell ourselves of how it was and is)
'INSIGHT STUDIES'

Tools of the South:
Soul doctoring tools including psychotherapy, hypnotherapy and all ways of understanding our personal mythology - our 'story' - and of healing the wounds of the emotional body and the past. We can group these tools under the general heading of 'Insight Studies'.

Looking at things in terms of energy, a past trauma is an energy knot, often felt somewhere in the solar plexus - belly area. Healing is a matter of undoing the knot until the energy is dissolved.

Tools of the West:
Ceremony is a powerful way of sending messages from the outer
to the inner. Through physical enactment in the outer world, such
as by setting up a Medicine Wheel with stones, marking the four
directions, and then facing the directions to make prayers (focus
intention) and to physically connect with water, earth, air and fire,
we can convey information to our Inner Being. Just as our Inner-
Being (so wrongly called subconscious or worse still unconscious,
mega-conscious would be more accurate.) speaks to our Outer-
Being in the language of the dreams, so we need to use that same
language to speak from the Outer to the Inner. Ceremony is a
vehicle for that.

Affirmations have become popular in the last 30 years or so and
they work up to a point. The advantage, however, of combining
them with ceremony is that ceremony adds the pictorial dream
language of the inner self and thus communicates more directly to
the Soul. A good ceremonial leader uses lots of theatre and
trappings to distract the everyday consciousness while the real
message goes in. In a sense one could say ceremony is three dimensional hypno-drama-therapy!

Earth awareness and dance-movement are ways of connecting
with the Earth of our-self. If we consider a human as centred in the
heart wheel, the lower world or earth world is all that is below -
the solar plexus centre, hara, and root chakras; and the upper
world is all that is above, the throat, third eye and crown. The West
relates to all that is below (and the East to all that is above) and so
the tools of the West are to help us connect to the Earth of our own
being and the earth herself.

Tools of the North:-
The Medicine Wheel teachings are ways to help us to understand
and 'frame' our world, to make the intense complexity of everyday
life more comprehensible and to make connection between that
and the subtle world of spirit.

Council is the Sacred Circle in which we share our inner life with each other and get to hear how it is for others inside themselves.

Shamanic journeys to the upper world are part of the movement of *'stopping the world'*. Meditation stills the everyday mind so we can open to spirit. Soul Retrieval is a profound way of journeying to retrieve lost aspects of our self.

Tools of the East:-

East is the place of the Magical Child and of rebirth, so here we have play - 'purposeless', timeless, creative activity - and vision quest, the placing of oneself in the natural world to receive vision from spirit.

Dance moves us from the West to the East in the movement from being in the here-now to the timeless, transformational place of ecstasy. Sexual healing methods belong on the West-East axis also.

The Centre:

In the Centre is The Great Mother, Mother Earth, Mother Nature, and The Great Father, Father Sun, around whom Mother Earth travels and a part of whose great solar system energy field she is. We come from the Earth and the Sun, we are their thinking children, we are their self-reflective brain cells.

BEING A WARRIOR - FOUR QUALITIES TO DEVELOP

PATIENCE AND PERSEVERENCE

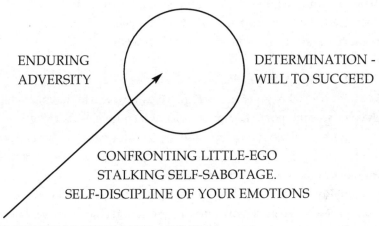

ENDURING
ADVERSITY

DETERMINATION -
WILL TO SUCCEED

CONFRONTING LITTLE-EGO
STALKING SELF-SABOTAGE.
SELF-DISCIPLINE OF YOUR EMOTIONS

UNBENDING INTENT TO AWAKEN

An experience of this wheel:
Many years ago, in my late teens, I was very moved by the traditional jazz music of New Orleans and I had some friends who
played musical instruments and had got a band together. The band
needed a clarinet so I bought one. I am not a natural musician but
I struggled with this awkward lump of wood and metal and kept
practicing, making so much terrible din that my landlady finally
asked me to practice elsewhere! When I was called up for National
Service I went with my suitcase in one hand and my clarinet, on
which I could, by then, squawk my way through a recognizable
tune, in the other. Little did I know, but this turned out to be a
major coup and during my 2 years in the army, my clarinet was an
incredible friend. I got off many parades, got special treatment in
all sorts of ways, and by the time I was demobbed I could actually
play passably. I formed a band back home and played semi-pro for
15 years in and around Liverpool. I was playing in the clubs of
Liverpool at the time the Beatles became popular and the Mersey
sound emerged nationally and then internationally. I was never
more than third rate but I got enormous pleasure and satisfaction

from actually achieving something which had seemed so improbable as I am not from a musical family and there was nothing in my background that supported me playing such non-classical and, at that time, almost underground music. This struggle to achieve took me around this wheel - especially perse-verance - and I learned many valuable lessons.

THE INNER SABOTEUR.

Most of us who grew up in the Western world have a well developed saboteur. That inner voice which knocks us to hell and back with its dialogue of put-downs, self-deprecation, 'never get anything right', 'never be any good'. Often these are parental injunctions or schoolteachers' criticisms internalized into a sub-personality which can become self-destructive and create dire unhappiness. We go deeply into this in Section One part 4, but here is one warrior's approach to the challenge:-

NO SUCH THING AS FAILURE TO A WARRIOR.

"I have always felt that although someone may defeat me, and I strike out in a ball game, the pitcher on the particular day was the best player. But I know when I see him again; I'm going to be ready for his curve ball. Failure is a part of success. There is no such thing as a bed of roses all your life. But failure will never stand in the way of success if you learn from it." - Hank Aaron, 1934, American Baseball Player.

It is important to maintain an attitude of success in all things. What is often called failure in ordinary terms is, from the point of view of a shaman, merely an additional challenge and opportunity to learn more!

FOUR HUMOURS OF THE SPIRITUAL WARRIOR

HUMOUR

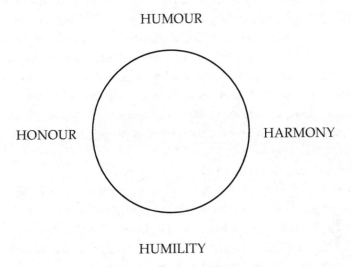

HONOUR   HARMONY

HUMILITY

To 'Walk Your Talk' as a Warrior of the Spirit, here are four very useful qualities.

Let there be HARMONY with Spirit, with the non-manifest worlds. Let yourself listen to the nudges, intuitions, and hunches sent by the Spirit-Beings and your personal guides of those worlds. Let Spirit influence your choices and guide your life.

HONOUR the Great Mother upon whose body you walk and out of whose body your physical vehicle is made. Honour that which creates and sustains all physical existence and gives this incredible gift of individual self-directed life, in which all actions bring reactions in the perfect feedback loop system of karma. Recycle your garbage with loving care

Approach emotions with HUMILITY, recognising that we are all children here at the Great Cosmic School of Mother Earth, engaged in learning through experience. We are all part of the Great ONE and we are contributing, each in our own way, to the evolution of THE ALL. Graduation is synonymous with full enlightenment, becoming a Master of Energy, someone whose inner and outer worlds match and who is always joyfully 'At

Cause' in the Great Vision Quest of Life.

Treat the realm of Mind with a touch of HUMOUR and don't let yourself get too serious about it all. Its good to remember that if the Creator did not have a sense of humour, we would not have a sense of humour. As above, so below. Things are meant to go 'wrong' - and 'right'. Without challenges and tests there is no story. With no story there is no hero or heroine. With no hero or heroine there is nothing gained, no achievement, no furtherance, no evolution. With no evolution there is no point to Creation.

A very short (and tall) story:-

James Bond was having a very, very good day. He had just completed his most challenging assignment ever and had dispatched all the baddies to gloriously horrible deaths. His favourite Bond-girls were ready and waiting at the Grandest Hotel but first he had an important appointment at the Secret Service HQ. He was welcomed by Moneypenny with a lingering kiss and by M with a hug. That's a touch unusual, he thought. Then M dropped a bit of a bombshell.

'James', he said graciously, 'you've done so magnificently that you have terminated all the enemies of the state. Smersh has given up and the Axis Of Evil has joined our side. An incredible achievement. There are no enemies any more and we no longer need spies so here's your P45, we're all out of a job and the service is being disbanded......

No film company would take up an option on that script!

Keep your eye on the cosmic joke..........

SHINING THE LIGHT OF CONSCIOUSNESS UPON ONESELF

The Great Journey Of Awakening begins when you first shine the 'light of awareness' upon your Self and ask yourself those awkward questions such as 'Who am I?, what's it all about?, why am I here? what am I living for?, what happens after I die?, what's the point of it all......???'

We turn around to face ourselves in the 'Mirror of Self-Reflection' and start to take on our-Self and our life as our own personal responsibility. Until then we tend to be governed by such things as how others see us, by the struggle for recognition, by lack of real self-esteem, by comparison of our self with others and with role-models, by comparing ourselves to 'celebrities', by emotional needyness and self-pity.

Here is a MEDICINE WHEEL OF DEPENDENCY!

2. Look at what I am doing.
See what I've done
Tell me I'm worthy.....

3. Do I look good? -
Are you sure?
Am I better looking
than him/her??
Tell me I look alright...
—- please.....

TELL ME WHO
I SHOULD BE...
Help ---
somebody tell me...

4. Tell me you accept
me REALLY?
You do accept me,
don't you??
Show me you
accept me - please....

1. Look at ME.
Am I OK? Really?
Are you sure??

These are attitudes and mind-sets that create enormous pain in life. The sum total of all that hinders us can be summed up as SELF-IMPORTANCE or perhaps one could call it self-obsession.

However, it is essential to remember that we are the most important person to our-self, that is a fact and it is natural. Our-Self is all we have. Freedom comes from getting away from dependence on how others see us and leaving them free to see us as they choose. They will anyway! How we see our-self is what is important and that depends on how honest we are with our-Self, how much integrity we have with our-self and how congruent our inner and outer lives are.

So where does all this come from? How did any of us get into this parlous state of dependency and lack of self worth?

We got INDOCTRINATED.........

THE WHEEL OF INDOCTRINATORS

PEER GROUP (ideas & concepts) INDOCTRINATORS

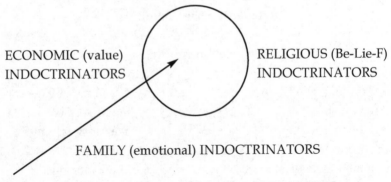

ECONOMIC (value)
INDOCTRINATORS

RELIGIOUS (Be-Lie-F)
INDOCTRINATORS

FAMILY (emotional) INDOCTRINATORS

POLITICAL (rights / lack of rights) INDOCTRINATORS.

The wheel shows the pressures and the conditioning put on us as we grew up, in order to attempt to form and control how we and our life developed. Most of us began under the thrall of everyday culture, governed by our needs for security, approval, recognition and acceptance. We will have been taught to look to the outside world for a sense of identity and to give away enormous amounts of our personal power and our right to self-direction.

How sad it is that such a state of affairs should be considered 'normal'. When I am giving a talk I often ask the people how many of them have ever been in a trance or been hypnotised. Some hands go up. I then ask how many think they have never been hypnotised. Usually quite a lot of hands go up, some very firmly. I then ask 'But what about the trance you are in right now?' I then talk about the deepest trance state on Planet Earth, the one we know as 'normal waking consciousness' and point out just how much of a conditioning it is. Usually there is laughter of recognition....

For some, this is a contentious and challenging idea, but just how conditioned are you? Just how conditioned, hypnotised, entranced are others you know?

Ever since we plopped out of the womb, we have been the subject of indoctrination. It is included in education, religion, upbringing, cultural conditioning, growing up into the 'right' sort of person, and it teaches us how to fit into the family and culture around us. Later in life we may travel to very different cultures and if we stay long enough, we can get a sense of how they see the world. Then the chances are good that we will get culture shock on the return home. This is a great opportunity to see just how 'normality' is a cultural phenomenon and not a given, and to see just how odd much that our own culture treats as normal really is.

THE INDOCTRINATORS
As we grow up it is the family who indoctrinate us into their ways, their mores, their framework of life, their rules and laws, prejudices and blindnesses. We are vulnerable and dependent and they, to us, are the 'gods' who know everything. So we learn all we can and we struggle to get it all right and be 'in with the in-crowd' of the family. We cannot afford to be 'out'. If the family lives in contradiction with itself, then we learn to do the same because, after all, they must be right, mustn't they. So we 'adopt' our parents ways and become like them as much as we can. We sell out, pretty much unconsciously, for the sake of our survival. We have to, there is not much choice.

This is how our emotional world is formed and this is where our conditioning begins.

Then in adolescence we start to rebel and we don't stand for the parental nonsense in the same way. We begin to differentiate and to criticize and to demand our own way, our own rules and our own views. Well, up to a point. This is when the peer group becomes all important and most of us are desperate to belong to it, so we sell out again to be part of that group.

The fashion industry and media affect greatly the 'norms' of that time of our life. Some might say the fashion industry control and we follow but I don't see it like that. Successful fashion designers catch on to a new emerging trend and push it for all they're worth, but they do not create it, as failed fashions demonstrate. It is interesting to reflect that the key to being 'fashionable' is nothing more than COPYING OTHER PEOPLE!

Our physical circumstances are governed by the economic indoctrinators. The media constantly bathe us in images of what is seen to constitute a successful person, the 'right' kind of lifestyle, house, car, job, wife/husband, hobbies, interests, fashions, food, drink, thoughts, feelings, pets, sayings.... When we try to be one of the in-people, while we are still 'empty' inside ourselves, we are vulnerable to this manipulation. But when we start to walk the Warrior's Path and to value Our-Self for our innate worth and not for what we have got or have achieved in the outer world, we become independent of this indoctrination and brainwashing and we gain personal power.

The spiritual aspect of life is/was controlled by the religious indoctrinators, the churches, who taught people what to believe. By giving over one's search and leaving it to them and believing what one was told, one could be 'saved' - saved from the difficult and tricky path of actually facing oneself and taking responsibility for one's own development. So self-discovery and self-development were subtly taught as unnecessary and a waste of time and effort. Just believe and it will all be done for you.....

The path of the Warrior of the Spirit, the search for the Holy Grail (The Real One - the one inside each and every one of us) was consigned to the dustbin and replaced by a set of ready-made beliefs and instructions. Just as junk food replaces the real thing with something effortless but worthless - though often quite palatable with its excesses of sugar, salt and strange chemicals - so real personal development, the real, tough, challenging and unflattering journey of personal evolution, was replaced by a façade of effortlessly simplistic, easy to take though actually self-negating beliefs, ready made to swallow and follow without thinking. Just believe what you are told and pledge yourself to the religious corporation, give your money, and you're soul will be taken care of. No matter how frightful the time you suffer on earth, you have the promise of eternal life sitting on the 'right hand of god' or some such mythical place - provided you do what you are told, obey all the injunctions, don't rock any boats and don't ask awkward questions. Many of our recent ancestors had that pushed down on them very powerfully. Many lost a lot of soul to those who sat in control and creamed off the wealth while the vast majority sweated at their behest.

In the Centre of this Wheel is the political indoctrinators, those to whom we are taught to give away the most power. No I don't mean the Conservatives, the Labour Party, the Republicans or Democrats, or any of them. Look behind these facades - which are not that much different from each other - and you find the indoctrinators of the culture, the powers who would like us to think we have a measure of control but actually who manipulate from hidden places out of sight, who control what constitutes 'education', cultural norms, ways of thinking, of framing life and lives. I could get into conspiracy theories here but that's for another time, though I must say I see them more as consummately ignorant, self-important attempts at domination for the benefit of the few at the expense of the many, which ultimately brings down the few as well. So in the end everyone loses.

SEXUALITY
Interestingly, here in the centre can also be placed our sexuality. What a strange combination you might think - sexuality and politics! But sexuality is a key driving force of most humans and the only way we get to be born, so those who would control us

seek to control it. There are two paths to world domination. One is with the 'sword' as by the empire building emperors and their conquering armies, the other is with the suppression of sexuality and its spontaneous natural expression, and with the mass-destruction weapons of shame and guilt, so beloved of religionists who implant these ideas into the psyche of the people for them to use against themselves. Suppress the vital force, make people think sex is somehow bad, tell them they are born in sin, tell them sexuality is only for procreation and not for enjoyment, tell them all the superior people - like the priests - don't do it.... In a word - brainwash them and set them against their very nature, and you have a suppressed population you can manipulate at will. Just look at European and Middle Eastern history. The Inquisition, for example. And not just history.....

This book is about consciousness and seeing what is so and what is not so and letting go of what does not serve, moving beyond the 'normal' brainwashed state of consciousness. We live in a time of male domination of money, power, religion, doctoring, and most things in most parts of the world. We live on a planet suffering greatly from the culmination of several thousand years of this male dominated warmongering, stupidity and ignorance, a planet whose structures are creaking badly as a result. Our children will see a time when the earth will cease to be able to function in her bountifulness and the great ignorance in these ideas of domination will reap their appropriate reward. Then these ways of thinking will be seen vividly to serve us no more. A great change is in the making.

WHEEL OF FASHION
and BEING 'IN' WITH THE IN-CROWD
('Empty' people's strategies)

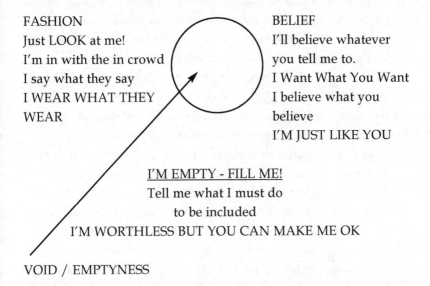

MEDIA
I can be a celebrity. I can be on
Oprah/Springer - just wait till you see
ME ON TV!

FASHION
Just LOOK at me!
I'm in with the in crowd
I say what they say
I WEAR WHAT THEY
WEAR

BELIEF
I'll believe whatever
you tell me to.
I Want What You Want
I believe what you
believe
I'M JUST LIKE YOU

I'M EMPTY - FILL ME!
Tell me what I must do
to be included
I'M WORTHLESS BUT YOU CAN MAKE ME OK

VOID / EMPTYNESS

Here is a wheel of what happens later after the indoctrinators have done their job. We become *fodder*, followers of fashion, loyal buyers of the latest goods, obedient consumers of what is hyped, willing believers in whatever the consensus tells us is true.

A BELIEVER - is one who - BE-(in-the)-LIE-(for)-EVER!
- Swiftdeer

Consider the extraordinary success of shows like Jerry Springer, Big Brother and the various celebrity TV nonsenses in which all sorts of people can be a 'celebrity' for a moment while they show themselves off on TV, frequently in their worst possible light for all to see. Incredible!

There is a horrible price for living in ignorance and if it doesn't come before, it comes in old age. Instead of becoming a wise and respected elder with years of valuable life experience to share for the benefit of the younger, you become treated as a piece of junk - in a retirement home - just waiting for death.

SEX AND 'NORMALITY'

Talking of INDOCTINATION - Isn't it WIERD that many of the commonly used words to describe the sexual act in the English language are also considered to be swear words? Doesn't that say volumes about the Anglo-Saxon attitudes to sexuality?

Consider the word 'fuck'. It comes from the 18th century when people were jailed for adultery and sexual misdemeanors and their 'crime' was labelled 'For Unlawful Carnal Knowledge' and abbreviated on the notice outside their cell to F.U.C.K.

Then there are the words bugger, wank, (get) stuffed, and so on.

The male organ is derogatorily known as prick, tool, willy, john-thomas, dick, etc, and the female organ as cunt (from cuni – latin for birth canal. Hence cuni-lingus), hole, pussy. All these words, even pussy, are generally used in a demeaning way or as something for a man's use at the expense of woman.

How come the words for our organs of lovemaking are all SO DEROGATORY, SO NEGATIVE, SO UNLOVING, SO DISRE-SPECTFUL?

How is it that our collective attitude towards the greatest act of creation any of us can do, the most potentially beautiful and pleasurable act any of us can experience and the most gloriously intimate act any of us can share should be regarded in such an extraordinarily negative way?

Isn't that TRULY PECULIAR??

Our sexual organs are our 'Weapons-Of-Mass-Creation' and we all are born through them – every single one of us only gets to be here through sex. Yet we collectively hold extraordinary disrespect for our beautiful organs of creation and the act through which our body-vehicles are created.

What about 'weapons of mass destruction'? We collectively hold no such reservations about them. Surely the really appalling things that happen to us are to do with war, killing, murder, ravaging, savagery, brutality, destruction, torture, decimation, genocide.....

So wouldn't it make more sense if our swear words reflected this?

Here are some suggestions for more relevant swear words:-

GET NUKED!
BOMB OFF!
EAT ANTHRAX!
GO JUMP ON A MINE!
GO PLAY ON THE RUNWAY!
TANK OFF- you tanker.
STUFF A TORPEDO UP YOUR ASS!
BLAST OFF!
GO AND RIDE A ROCKET!
I'LL GENETICALLY MODIFY YOU!
MAY THE EVIL EMPIRE GET YOU!
NUKE 'EM TILL THEY GLOW!
                    Feel free to add your own!

ATTITUDES

Useful attitudes for a Spiritual Warrior.

There are many common attitudes that do not serve our evolution but merely conspire to keep us stuck and afraid. Here are two very useful ways of looking at common daily issues. Firstly....

THE WHEEL OF MISTAKES

Focused INTENT -
to learn from mistakes

3 PRESENCE OF MIND   5. Cultivate the   4 SPIRITUAL
to learn from the   ABILITY to learn   PERCEPTION -
mistakes of others   without mistakes.. to learn from mistakes
                                           of your teachers

1. OPEN HEART
Dare to learn by making
as many mistakes as you need.

'A Warrior accepts that mistakes are Great Teachers and thus learns not to fear them.....'

Osho (Bhagwan) Rajneesh used to say something like this to his disciples. 'I tell my sannyasins to make lots of mistakes every day. But not to make the same old ones again and again. Everyday go out and make new mistakes!'

The real skill is to learn from other people's mistakes, your teacher's mistakes and ultimately without mistakes at all. But meanwhile in the land of ordinary mortals, most of us have to make our own mistakes before we get the lesson. So.....

With an open heart, dare to learn, accept that you will make mistakes and let there be no blame, no shame and no guilt.

Approach with an attitude of readiness to learn from

experience. Seek the wisdom to never repeat your mistakes, but if you do – learn the lesson even better.

In daily life, be PRESENT to learn from life and from other people's mistakes. It is a lot less painful than making your own.

Be aware that no teacher is perfect. Learn from your teacher but allow them their imperfections. Take the learning with you but leave their personality traits and foibles behind.

To learn without mistakes is a great achievement and ability.

LIKED AND DISLIKED

DISLIKE

HATE   UNCONDITIONAL   LOVE
Unreasonable   LOVE   Beyond logical
antipathy   Don't care at all   reason

LIKE

The second teaching is about the issue of being liked or disliked. Some of us have been taught that if everyone doesn't love us or like us, there must be something wrong with us - that we should expect to be liked by everyone.

Well, human beings do not all vibe the same and do not all have the same intent for this incarnation. We are a mixed bunch of beings at different stages and in different aspects of evolution. And who is to say we are even here to learn the same kind of things? It is very helpful to recognize that we are gloriously diverse within our basic human commonality, and this Wheel of Like and Dislike can help towards a sense of freedom from the very self-condemnatory idea that 'everyone SHOULD LIKE ME or else there is something WRONG WITH ME'.

Consider that out of the totality of humans that you come across in life, perhaps one fifth - 20% or so - will fall naturally into each category

This medicine wheel teaches that we do not need to put ourselves through the pain of trying forlornly to be loved by all because it is never going to happen. Freedom is letting go of expectations, letting go of unnecessary self-judgments and judgments of others. It is freeing to just accept that other humans will react to us in all possible ways and those who it is our destiny to walk and work with will like and love us just as we naturally and instinctively like and love them.

A very important thing about this medicine wheel is that UNCONDITIONAL LOVE and DON'T CARE AT ALL are a mere hair's breadth apart. But that hair's breadth is totally important and makes 100% difference. To love unconditionally means to love without concern for the outcome, just to love - irrespective of everything. To not-care is also to have no concern for the outcome. The difference is that the one holds the quality of lovingness and the other doesn't. Ordinary human love is conditional and depends on a response and contains an expectation within it. Unconditional love is different and is perhaps best expressed as 'lovingness', AGAPE in Greek. It is to hold the object of your love with lovingness quite irrespective of whether you receive anything back whatsoever. Responsibility for children is the greatest teacher of this quality.

ALLIES AND ENEMIES

WISDOM & KNOWLEDGE
Dogmatic clarity. bullshit and stupidity

INTROSPECTION
old age and death
Inertia - deadness
Lack of self
knowledge

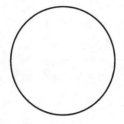

INSPIRATION
ILLUMINATION
Fantasy of self
importance
- misuse of power

TRUST & INNOCENCE
Fear, inhibition, shyness, lack of self worth

An 'ALLY' is a quality that will help and guide you towards manifestation of your highest good, of your gifts and talents and of your 'dream' of a good life.

An 'ENEMY' is a quality that will challenge you and try to trip you up, hook you to self-importance, and keep you in the slavery of little ego.

Remember both are equal and equally necessary. Always bless your enemies because it is they who push you to bring forth the best of yourself.

Allies and Enemies of the South

Through honest 'close to' work on our emotional body, we learn to gain the ability to trust. Trust is not a simple matter because naive trust, easy trusting, never served anyone in this complex, tricky and coyote-ridden world. 'Trust in the Lord and tether your camel', goes the old Bedouin saying. But we can learn real trust though feed-back, through life experience, through test and response. We learn when to trust, who to trust, and when the hunch we are feeling is the spirit speaking and not just good old wishful thinking, coyote-on-the-make, little self-serving ego doing its best to disguise itself.

Innocence - or inner sense - inner essence - means being in clear contact with one's inner place. Through openness with our inner feeling centre, and thus the ability to trust our-Self, we can gain the ability to know what and who to trust in the outer world. Thus to live with trust and innocence is to live with inner trust and inner sense which enables one to live with outer trust and sense through the ability to discriminate.

The primary enemy of the South is emotional fear, shyness, inhibition, the knot in the stomach which stops us in our tracks. This fear is about feeling unable to trust oneself in a situation and it is a powerful enemy for many people that chronically inhibits the quality of life. It is an enemy to be confronted at every turn and vanquished. To have no inhibitions whatsoever does not mean to throw off one's clothes and do silly inappropriate embarrassing (em-bare-ass-ing!) things. It simply means to have choice over your actions and not to be controlled and limited by your past or by other people's views on how you should be or who you should be. Imagine the joy of having no shyness whatsoever and thus being free to choose how to act in any moment without emotional fear. That's freedom!

The way this enemy manifests is usually repetitive self-pitying stories and 'pain games' with which we 'entertain' ourselves and excuse ourselves from confronting challenges, taking responsibility, and actually growing up and tackling the stuff of our lives. And isn't it so much easier to catch other people doing this than oneself?

Allies and Enemies of the North

The North quality of wisdom and knowledge is about living with an ever-open mind. Real knowledge is gained through experience of life. Listening to other people can guide and help you but believing what they tell you without personal experience leads to dogma and the enemy of 'clarity' i.e. bullshit. Knowledge is NEVER gained from belief - belief is the enemy of knowledge. I am going to say this again -

BELIEF IS THE ENEMY OF KNOWLEDGE

And I am not alone in this. -
"The greatest enemy of the truth is not lies but firmly held beliefs." -
Schopenhauer

"Belief, in fact, is every human's greatest foe. More people have believed what life is than people who have learned what life is".
Estcheemah (shamaness) quoted by Hyemeyhosts Storm in *Lightningbolt* (pp267)

I am being pedantic because Coyote is out there in miriad disguises saying 'believe-in-me, trust-in-us, give us your power, invest your money in this sure-fire winner, let me make up your mind for you, let me sign your cheques or better still just give me your chequebook to look after; surrender to me - a spiritual master - worship at my one true altar; the 'only son of god' is our property and unless you worship through us you are doomed, we are god's holy chosen people and anyone who crosses us is an enemy of god (so convenient), we bring the one true god to the heathens and until they are converted they are subhuman so it is our right and duty to conquer them, take their lands, enslave them and 'save' them - and all for their own good' - of course......
Belief has been peddled in so many ways, but belief beggars any possibility of real knowledge, growth and wisdom. The very act of becoming 'a believer' is an act of saying 'I will close my mind to any further information which conflicts with this dogma I have chosen to accept'. This is truly 'selling your soul to the devil'. It prevents any connection with the real Creator who IS The Creation in which we and all living things exist as Co-Creators, Aspects of Creation. The price is nothing less than your freedom - and people everywhere seem to be looking for something or someone to pay this diabolical price to. Anything to save them from self-responsibility, the responsibility of making and standing by their own choices, the responsibility and right to create and live their own lives in their own way, the right to explore and learn through

experience just what really is and is not.

Beliefs are like viruses!
They get into our brains and delete our natural instinctual knowing.

Have you ever listened to a fully domesticated, consensus-reality believer trotting out all those socially correct bullshit views? All that stuff that we have been taught to parrot, all those ideas that the system inculcates into us if it can. All those ideas and concepts that keep a person robotized and unable to think for himself?

One of the saddest people I ever met was a man I knew in my (and his) early twenties who was a pillar-of-society type with the right accent, right modest conservative clothes, right attitudes and all that. Just the sort of person I presumed would become a success. I met him again in our mid-sixties at a reunion. He had lived the 'right kind of life', believed and done all the 'right things'. His pension had been stolen from him by company default and his government pension was quite inadequate. He had retired from his sensible career and all his sensible plans had led him to an inability to maintain any kind of decent lifestyle in his retirement. He was on anti-depressants plus a cocktail of other pills to sort out the side effects and the further side effects. He had believed in the system, done the 'right things', obeyed the cultural norms and the strictures that the system had taught him, and the place it got him to was one of misery and despair in old age. VERY SAD.

Remember – the 'system' is there for itself and its controllers/beneficiaries, NOT FOR YOU!

Belief And Cults
A cult is what happens when a group of people come together around an idea that then becomes a belief system, often galvanised by a charismatic leader to whom the members give their power - and usually money too.

The essential uniting quality of a cult is a belief so firmly held that sometimes the cult members will even die to maintain it. The word cult is bandied about today and applied to any group with views differing from the mainstream. This is quite wrong – a cult is always about a belief so firmly held that it must be defended at all costs. Hence, the tendency for earthy common sense to go right out of the window and cult members to do quite extraordinary and even horrific things in the interests of the 'good' of the cult.

This is also the definition of some religions too – the concept that belief must be the cornerstone of what is held sacred. Hence jihads, hence crusades. Our more ancient ancestors would have found such ideas quite absurd. They explored to find out through experience, to learn by trial and error. Their ways - which have come down to us as 'shamanism' and 'paganism' and under other titles too such as 'heathen' (the divine seen in the heath, in nature) and witchcraft (the craft of the wise woman) have come from their exploration over tens of thousands of years and are guidelines for us to try out and see if they work for us. They are not for us to believe willy-nilly or to take on and suspend our faculties of discernment. They are tools for us to use to explore Life, the Universe and Everything, to find out, to test, to learn, to increase the fund of human knowledge through our experience.

Some practitioners of science are dogmatic believers too, deter-mined that they have all the answers. It is good to remember that a skeptic is a believer, often seriously dogmatic and closed. To disbelieve is also a belief!

Allies and Enemies of the East
The allies of the East are inspiration, illumination and enlight-enment. It is the place of coming into the light and finding the magic moment of 'AHA!' That moment brings a sense of power, clarity and knowledge, and it is at that moment that we are faced with choosing how we use that power. Do we use it in service as 'craft' or do we use it as 'macht', might, power to manipulate a situation or a person to our advantage?

It is through human choice that we create good and evil. We are faced with this choice everyday in miriad forms in a multitude of moments. How do we act in the world? Do we act with integrity, knowing that the ultimate good of all is our highest aim? Or alternatively, do we sneak a bit of advantage here and there, living with spiritual pride, self-glorifying misuse of power, rejection of the Earth and matter and attachment to 'superior spiritual affairs'?

This is the daily, hourly, minute-ly challenge of the East.

THE SECRET IN 'THE SECRET'.

The idea that we can *create our own reality* is popular in self-development circles in many developed (rich) countries. I remember back in the late seventies when I first went to live in California, all sorts of otherwise intelligent people firmly believed that chain letters were a path to prosperity. The fact that no value is added and that money is merely transferred from the late comers in the chain to the early birds escaped rational consideration. I think this idiocy has now pretty much been seen for what it is, but there is another 'path to prosperity' which, though much more worthy, calls now for a touch of extra light to be shone upon it. This is contained in 'The Secret' and many other books on manifesting your desires.

In a rich country, it is relatively easy to manifest your desires especially when the current means of exchange is printed pieces of paper. The government simply prints more and we are all 'richer', borrowing is easy, debt is the way to "wealth"; we can have it all now, whatever 'it' is. The western world has been in a massive twenty-five year bull market of increasing affluence, fuelled in the last 10 years by cheap goods from the Far East and ever increasing amounts of funny-munny – printed paper and entries in computer ledgers. ('Artificial Economics'). The emperor of the world – the USA – is the chief debtor of the world. Empires only last while they are creditors and certainly not when they are the major world debtor of all time*. Remember the Roman Empire – it collapsed when its credit was no longer respected.

---

*See 'The World Factbook' published by the C.I.A. at -

www.cia.gov/library/publications/the-world-factbook/rankorder/2187rank.html and prepare to be surprised.

The techniques for drawing your desires to you are described in such books as 'The Secret' and 'The Cosmic Ordering Service' and they have value, but with some serious caveats. Reading the words of some 'prosperity teacher/gurus' I feel the real message has got distorted by the assumptions of a wealthy culture accustomed to ease and plenty and the idea that wealth can be 'drawn to you effortlessly' just by a 'positive' attitude, all rather reminiscent of chain letter economics! It is good to remember that we can only draw to us in material terms from what is available out there. Life works on the basis of exchange and if some take more but give less, others end up without enough. (Just look at the imbalances between countries) In many an ancient culture people were revered for what they gave, not what they took. This change is a serious reversal of ancient wisdom and we are not the better for it. There is an important paradox too in that our real deep happiness and joy in life comes from what we give and not what we take, so all ideas aimed at 'getting what you want out of it' have an innate flaw and need to be understood as products of a kind of capitalist influenced spirituality which values 'success' in terms of acquiring and having more.

For a real grounded look at prosperity and wealth, we need to look at nature. Everything goes in cycles from abundance to shortage and back again. Often when there is a shortage of some things, others are plentiful instead. The animal kingdom under-stands this completely and lives through their ability to sense what is coming and adapt. We humans try to distort and override nature's cycles, but we cannot eradicate them. Twenty five years is a very long bull (growth) phase as the norm is more like four years. We need to stay awake as change is coming our way and we cannot take easy wealth for granted, particularly as we have given away much of our manufacturing (i.e. value-adding) base to the countries of the Far East.

We do not create our own reality, that is human hubris – the idea we are top of the tree and everything else in creation is just here for us - and an experience of a substantial earthquake will probably convince you (It did me!), but we do influence reality and we are entirely responsible for our own interpretation of reality and our own actions resulting from that interpretation - and the future we co-create via those actions.

Allies and Enemies of the West

The quality of introspection is the quality of knowing deeply one's inner self, the Inner Spirit Being who *'dreams'* the outer life we are living.

The final enemy is old age and death, and this comes to us all, though how it comes is a matter of great import and a result of how we have lived our life. It is very directly a result of how much we have developed our inner spiritual life because when the outer garment falls away, it is then that we discover what we have left.

During our lifetime this enemy expresses itself as inertia or deadness, tendencies to self absorption, self obsession, lack of joy and sense of purpose, and ultimately as depression when the self retreats within, unable to cope with the external life.

The ultimate struggle of the WEST is between the ally of daring to look deeply within and face whatever you find there - and thereby become master of it - and the enemy of what happens when you avoid the truth of who you are and of your mortality.

IT IS A 'LIFE' (ALIVENESS) AND 'DEATH' (DEADNESS) STRUGGLE!

Current lack of inner knowledge and lack of success with the inner struggle is reflected in the outer creation of a world suffering ecological destruction and war.

Cycle of Enemies

This cycle is very useful to know.

DEPRESSION	6th chakra
STRESS	5th chakra
ANGER	4th chakra
FEAR	3rd chakra

This is a map of the everyday enemies, the challenges we encounter. A situation occurs in life and it generates fear - anxiety - a little movement of energy in the solar plexus or 3rd chakra. If we deal with that situation, fine, the fear goes away and we go on to the next challenge. If not, there can be trouble in store. The energy moves up to the heart wheel, the 4th chakra, and is felt as anger. Anger is love, desire, the wish for unity - denied its expression. The heart is closed and anger is felt because love is denied. Anger is a call to action to restore unity and lovingness. Anger calls us to right a wrong.

If we express our feelings and succeed in putting things to rights, and unity restored, fine. But if not, then more trouble. We may find ourselves dropping things, bumping into things, having minor accidents or even major ones. We can find our energy level low and our irritability level high. This is all a sure sign we are denying our feelings to our self and action is needed to find out from our inner self what is really going on. Lots of illnesses result from this kind of denial as the unexpressed energy which is designed to change an outer situation goes toxic and acts against the self. Diseases like arthritis, cancer and M.E. can have roots here.

If anger does not find its rightful expression, the energy goes up to the 5th chakra, the throat, and is felt as stress, tension, dry throat. Muscular rigidity tends to set in. Chronic stress is a major problem for a lot of people. This means we need to do all we can to express our feelings, vocalise, release - and if we can do that and put the situation to rights, then things can become OK again, the energy is moved and the system moves towards equilibrium.

If not, then real trouble. Chronic stress leads to depression. The energy goes up to the third eye (6th charka) and closes it down to the outer world. This is the retreat into withdrawal. We have been unable to put things to rights in the outer world and the only thing left is to retreat into the inner world. Depression is the Self attempting to rebalance its-Self, taking time out to re-organize inside. It needs to be honoured as a necessary step in healing. The penalties for invalidating depression are far worse than the depression itself. Extreme failure here can lead to a splitting of the personality into seemingly separate fragments.

After a period of exhaustion or perhaps illness – which is Spirit's way of forcing us to take a period of rest and renewal - the person will be able to venture out again to confront the fear that they were unable to deal with in the first place, and so the cycle repeats. Hopefully, this time with more self knowledge and more self care than before, the person succeeds and takes the necessary action to deal with the cause that started the whole cycle in the first place.

ON A LARGER SCALE - TERRITORY, DOMINANCE AND

EMPIRE.

Many male predator animals live in a 'fuck-or-fight' universe, one of battles and territorial dominance, power over others or lose out. We humans are still quite stuck in this primitive simple mindedness and for maybe 4-6000 years (perhaps longer) now, since concepts of male domination and owning the earth swept over human society, we have created empires based on just such narrow thinking. It is worthwhile noting that EVERY EMPIRE, all the way from Gilgamesh to the British Empire, HAS FALLEN! The current 'emperors' – the Americans - are clearly approaching the end of their time right now and are behaving with reckless abandon, as have many empires before in their death throes. For all our advancement in the ways of science and the manipulation of outer material things, we still have an enormously long journey of inner development to travel to learn to live in co-operation and harmony with each other and our one-and-only planet-home. We have yet to develop a working-together global consciousness and it is going to take a lot of serious effort emotionally and spiritually to achieve that before our tampering with the ecology of the earth pushes a number of us to an early demise. This is the biggest challenge of the 21st century.

It is urgent now to put our fragmented world view, our fragmented concept of Creator/Creation and our fragmented selves back together again.

THE FOUR LODGES

Medicine of the Animal totems

HORSE/BUFFALO/WOLF/DRAGON
THE *KNOWING* PLACE

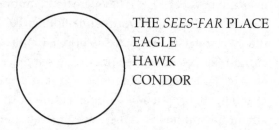

THE *LOOKS-*
WITHIN PLACE
GRIZZLY BEAR
OWL,
JAGUAR

THE *SEES-FAR* PLACE
EAGLE
HAWK
CONDOR

THE *CLOSE-TO* PLACE
MOUSE / COYOTE
SERPENT

A Lodge is, in this sense, a place or 'home', but inner home rather than anything external. It is where our spirit, our essence dwells, and typically we will find that one of the four directions is just that – it is 'home' for us, and its challenges are easy and its gifts are natural and plentiful. Two other directions may be challenging and perhaps difficult at times, but we are likely to find that most of the work we need to do is the fourth direction.

The *CLOSE-TO* place of the South is where we must attend to our-Self and what is right before us. It is the medicine of Little Mouse who lives close to the ground and sees what is right before his nose. We humans need to begin most of our endeavours in the South by attending to our own needs first. Our own actual <u>needs</u>, not necessarily our desires, wants and wishes. We attend to the needs of the child within and listen to what is 'close-to'. It is the quality of attention to life's little details, to what is under our feet and before our eyes that enables us to build a solid foundation for work in the other three directions.

There is a lot of guilt-creating nonsense talked about being altruistic and giving-away all the time as if to justify one's right to exist - a sort of injunction to 'Love thy neighbour but if you love yourself you are seriously wierd'. This has been pushed onto women, in particular, in this still primarily-patriarchal society. Altruism is a wonderful quality, but if practiced to an individual's detriment, it is no longer of benefit to anyone. The problem is that 'empty' people have nothing to give. All of us at times in our lives are empty people. At those times we need to receive, we need support, assistance, love and caring. And first of all we need to be able to give to our-self because if we cannot do that it is very hard for anyone else to give to us. Then when we are full enough we can give back to others and thus the circle is completed. But it is good to remember that it is a circle and giving and receiving are equal in importance. When we are full, we can give freely and joyfully. And without someone who can happily receive, we cannot enjoy the beauty of giving.

The south is also the realm of 'Coyote the Trickster'. It is Coyote who brings people to the Path, to all paths of change and development, to all ways of facing self and to the awareness of the need for mastery of the self. It is Coyote who makes sure that things go sufficiently 'wrong' for Consciousness to keep awake and keep evolving, and for us humans to be kept on our toes of awareness. It is Coyote who lays waste the most careful plans and who brings the most unexpected amazing failures and catastrophes, successes and joys, and whose speciality is bringing monstrous egos down to earth!

Serpent is an animal of the South in Inca mythology. Serpent sheds his skins and thus teaches us about the need to shed ours, to shed our box-of-life when it has outworn its usefulness and to have the courage to move on and to keep learning.

The LOOKS-WITHIN place of the WEST is the realm of Bear. Grandmother-Grandfather Grizzly Bear hibernates though the winter and looks deep within and dreams. This is the place of the inner, the dark, the deep, where the compost mulches and new creation begins. It is the womb of life, the deep feminine, where we all must go to meet our creativity, our wellspring. It is the place where we learn about our real self, the one we meet when we are alone in the night with nothing and no one. It is the self that is left when all the trappings, glories, glamours, and illusions have fallen away.

West is the place of old age, death and change. It is the feminine place, the intuitive place, the place of the Grandmothers, of woman, of the Great Mother, Mother Earth. It is the place Western society most tries to avoid - it is the place of greatest suffering in our world today with the polluting and wanton destruction of the natural infrastructure of our mother planet and the lack of honour given to woman by political structures and religions in many parts of the world.

We cannot know our-self without looking within. We cannot make sense of external life without knowing the life within. We cannot enjoy the light of the East without knowing the dark of the West. We cannot creatively and joyfully express the masculine outer self in the external world without the understanding, balance and foundation of the feminine inner self. Depression – as discussed in the last chapter - an 'enemy' of the West, teaches the power of *Looks-Within* to those who resist entering deeply enough into this realm of their own free will.

Owl is also a power animal of the West. Owl is Nightbird and bringer of the dream. Jaguar is the Inca totem for the West and teaches of the need to become a spiritual Warrior in order to gain the sobriety to face death.

The NORTH is the *KNOWING-PLACE*. It is the place of mind, of thinking, calculating, working out, pricing, valuing. accounting, reasoning, theorising, planning and philosophising. Have you ever considered how much time you spend valuing, pricing, bargain hunting, calculating? The almightly dollar (as it used to be), the not-quite-so-almighty pound sterling, the peso, peseta, rand, crown, franc, mark, euro... - the value-gods of our world - they eat up an amazing amount of our collective time and energy!

North is the place of clarity of mind and it is nice to be clear about things - to have the joy of clarity - but oh! how quickly that clarity can turn into know-all certainty and dogma. Clarity is a treacherous ally and is best treated with a strong sense of humour. When you really, really, finally are completely convinced you know absolutely just what's what and just what precisely you are doing and why and just exactly what will happen as a result, that's the moment Coyote is waiting for and you can be sure he is loaded and ready!

Buffalo is one of the animals of the North and buffalo knows his place in the scheme of things. He knows that he gives, so the people may live. Buffalo gives all of himself. It is good to remember that we too give all of ourselves in the final account as nothing can be taken from this realm except our experiences of life and love.

Horse is also a totem animal of the North and is revered as the keeper of knowledge and philosophy. The image of the white horse in all his glory, power and knowing is a wonderful image of North-power of balance, harmony and alignment. Wolf is a power animal of the North too and is seen as teacher, pathfinder and keeper of the family. Dragon is an Inca totem of the North and brings us to a moment of 'Stopping The World' and experiencing 'Direct Knowing'.

The EAST is the *SEES-FAR* place and is the realm of Eagle, Hawk and Condor. Eagle flies high and is messenger to and from the gods of the upper world of the sky. The East is the place we go to see the big picture, to get an overview, to seek a sense of illumination about what is going on. It is when we get to the East, after travelling South, West and North, that we may reap the benefits of our journey and enter an 'aha' moment of revelation, a moment in the Light.

The East is the masculine place of illumined action in the external world and is thus in complete balance with the feminine intuitive place of the West. Ideally that is. Just as the West out of balance is the realm of inertia and depression, so the East out of balance is the realm of misused power. This is power gone out of balance and seeking control over others, over Mother Earth's resources, seeking control of the environment, over all things known and unknown. The control freak with his guns and his army running riot over the Great Mother trying to ensure his safety and security by massacring all who could possibly be a threat - the paranoid schizophrenic, the psychopath - or am I just talking about some of the world leaders, kings and queens and religious fanatics of the last few thousand years?

The East is the direction of vision and *seeing-far* and so is the place of choosing and determining. When we make our life choices with attention to our spirit, our inner essence, inner voice, we are likely to make creative guided choices from a broader view and for the good of more than just little self.

Feel into these descriptions and how they speak to you. Which directions are familiar and easy to you and which pose more of a challenge?

THE RED ROAD AND THE BLUE ROAD

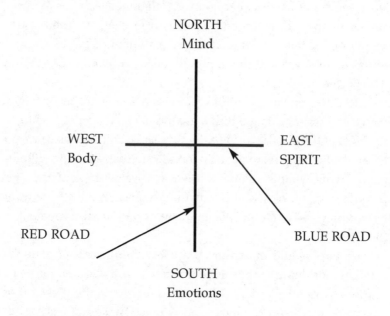

The RED ROAD is the North-South axis of mind and emotions
The BLUE ROAD is the West-East axis of body and spirit

To walk the Warrior's Path we walk BOTH roads simultaneously. We walk the RED ROAD to heal the emotional wounds of the past and move beyond the mental bondage of unfounded beliefs. Until we heal old resentments, bitterness, suppressed feelings and so on, they will go with us around our wheel of life and wreak their havoc. Life does not let us off anything, we have to face all the stuff of our past.

We walk the BLUE ROAD to still the body (and thus the mind and emotions) so we can open up consciousness to multi-dimensional reality. We can then travel in other realms to find guidance and help to understand who and what we really are and to gain a deeper understanding of the real meaning and purpose of our life.

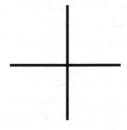

Together the two roads make a cross. This is the cross on which the 'Christ' – every one of us as the sons and daughters of Great Spirit - is 'crucified' i.e. limited, restricted and contained on entering matter. As free spirit we take on the limitation of gross matter, our earth body 'vehicle of experience'. As we all know, it can be a painful vehicle to be in! And a joyous one too. We are constantly asked to release, let go, let God – the Source – be our guide and, in effect, live through us. Yet we struggle with Little-Ego, with our self-importance, with the traumas of our personal history, and we are all deeply affected by cultural and human history. This is our life arena, and the Great Feedback Wheel of Karma – action brings reaction – constantly teaches us and does not let us off the hook.

In the Jesus myth, as in the earlier similar myths of Mythras, Attis, Osiris, Dionysos, Adonis, Horus and many others, it is the ego which gets crucified on the cross (not a person) so that the Spiritual-Self awakens. This is the aim of all spiritual paths - to die to the little self so the Source can manifest though us.

THE LIVED LIFE AND THE UNLIVED LIFE

All of us have the life we have lived and the other one – the life we sought but just somehow failed to get to grips with and make real – the unlived life. So what happened?

What CALLINGS passed us by, what NUDGES OF SPIRIT did we ignore?

Years ago when I ran a factory manufacturing metal containers, I exhausted myself. Anyone who has run a small business will know how easy that is to do. I reached an impasse. I was struggling with the business and working all hours trying to make up for the loss of 50% of sales due to the major customer's change to plastic. My personal life was a non-event. A number of strange things happened that suggested all was not OK but it wasn't until, before my eyes, a large chunk of the factory roof fell in, that I got the message. It felt as if the roof was falling in on my life. Only then did I put the essential changes in motion. My unlived life was calling and it called hard.

it is a long way from Managing Director of a manufacturing business to student/teacher/ facilitator/writer in the field of shamanism and personal development, and I had no idea whatsoever that the journey would lead here or anywhere like it, only that I had to do something to heal my wounded, grieving, lost self.

I was lucky. Due to the changes in culture, the human potential-spiritual awareness 'New Age' movement (call it by what names you will) was emerging and I could find others in search of meaning and find guidance towards a better way of life. In earlier times there was no such hope and people were bound by cultural mores, belief systems, the domination of religion, the should, must and ought of a shackled and bound society, heaped with guilt by the bucket-load on anyone who would not conform to the norms. The toxic force of fear has been weakened in the last 40 to 50 years. Let us see that it does not regain such a foothold again.

THE WARRIOR AND THE EGO
The inner battleground

Hidden within, behind the veil of the ego and its games, behind its fears, insecurities, past memories and unhealed traumas, lies the True-Self. Little-Ego fears the True-Self because True-Self shows it all the inadequacies that it is hell-bent on hiding, especially from its-self. When True-Self shines a light, Little-Ego can no longer blame everybody and everything else for its woes, all those people in its history such as parents, siblings, teachers and governments for all its failings and its hurts and pains. True-Self is spiritual and connected, while Little-Ego is separate and alone. True-Self co-operates with evolution while Little-Ego grasps for involution - just me, me, me and mine, mine, mine. True-Self walks in Beauty into the future while Little-Ego hangs on rigidly to the past.

The way that the Warrior, the True-Authentic-Self, sees the world and the way the ego sees the world form the inner battle-ground. In the struggle for inner supremacy that is fought within each of us, two very conflicting world views wage war in full combat. The thing is - Little Ego is a very scared being and he is terrified of letting-go - of almost anything!

LITTLE-EGO 'S BELIEF SYSTEM

I am separate and alone, and so is everyone else.

We are all competing for a limited supply of what is available.

External reality is what is and all that is. It is out there and I have to struggle with the day-to-day of it.

Self preservation comes first. There is only one life and I must make the most of it. At the end I will die and that will be pretty much that.

God is somewhere else (if there is one), and is busy fighting

Satan and all the bad guys on my behalf because I am too puny to do it for myself.

I am separate from God and its up to me to believe in Him if I want any sort of eternal life (which there isn't anyway but I feel better when I kid myself)

The WARRIOR'S (Soul's / True-Self's / Authentic Self's) UNDERSTANDING

We are all one and we are different aspects of HU-MAN-ITY. Humanity is just one part of existence.

There is abundance if we co-operate to share it around. Mother Earth gives enough for all.

External reality is only part of what exists. The dream-world or inner-world is more real and affects what we later experience in the outer world as effect.

There is no separate self to preserve as we are eternal beings. We are each part of the unity of consciousness and existence.

God is here, now, and everywhere, for always. We live inside God as part of God.

A GOOD WORD FOR EGO

We all need an ego to function well and the better and more developed our ego, the better we can function in the everyday. It is most important not to dismiss the ego but to develop him to do his job well. He is a necessary servant for our everyday adult persona, but he is not a good master. It is a matter of who is in charge. If we live from our warrior-self / authentic self / soul-self - we can 'Walk The Beauty Way' in peace and harmony and ego can serve us to steer a good course through the everyday stuff of life. If ego is in charge he will tell us all sorts of untruths because he is terrified to lose control and he knows he will if we grow up and become spiritual warriors, true to our authentic selves. Furthermore he knows it will be a death sentence for him if we really get to the truth.....

So he tries to maintain control, control, control.

Oh Little-Ego, don't you just love being in

CONTROL! CONTROL! CONTROL!!

--- --- --- --- --- --- --- --- --- --- --- --- --- --- --- --- --- --- ---

THE TRUE WARRIOR VALIDATES SELF.

A warrior doesn't let criticism get to her,
does not respond reflexively without thinking,
does not let her energy be deflated
does not take her life too personally.

A warrior is strong in self-knowledge and maintains self-approval irrespective of whatever projections are thrown at her.
A warrior does not let others define her or affect her sense of reality.
She maintains personal sovereignty.

While Little-Ego wants constant re-assurance he is OK,
the Warrior knows that others' approval comes and goes,
that it is largely ephemeral and, like celebrity, blows with the winds,
so she doesn't take any of it personally,
and she remains centred within Herself.

PART 3: THE 'MOVERS'

THE NON- CARDINAL DIRECTIONS

ENLARGING THE MAP.

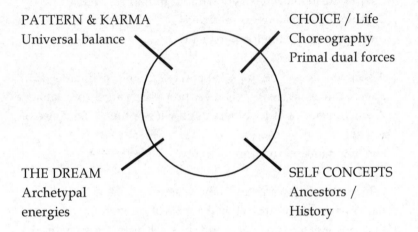

PATTERN & KARMA
Universal balance

CHOICE / Life
Choreography
Primal dual forces

THE DREAM
Archetypal
energies

SELF CONCEPTS
Ancestors /
History

Whilst the four cardinal directions are the 'fixed' energies or HOLDERS of the medicine wheel, the non-cardinals are the 'MOVERS' of energy.

THE SOUTHEAST DIRECTION
   Between the East: Spirit - fire - timeless
   And the South: Water - emotion - past

 is the Southeast place of THE ANCESTORS and OUR HISTORY.

This means all that has gone before now from which comes what is present here.

OUT OF SPIRIT AND INTO WATER!

We come out of the freedom and intangibility of spirit into the watery realm of the womb and the body to be born into the third dimension of material reality. With us comes the genetic history of our newly created 'vehicle of experience', and also the experiences of our spirit essence and past incarnations. We come from the spirit realm to be born into the garden of earthly delights and individual experience and we are given an earth-vehicle to live in for the duration.

We bring with us, deep in our unconscious, the experience of all our past incarnations, our lives, our deaths, our successes and our failures, what we have learned and what we have failed to learn that we have contracted to face this time around. Added to that is the genetic history of our 'vehicle of experience', our human ancestry and the mould of our vehicle's family of origin, the ancestral burdens and gifts of our human line.

Imagine yourself sitting in the Southeast of your wheel:

You sit in the place of your ancestry, history and all the forces that have moulded you to become the person that you are at this moment.

To your right is your spirit-self, your fire, your timeless eternal being, the source from which your consciousness came and where your past life experience is located.

To your left is your inner child, that which your consciousness of this lifetime first became. Southeast is the direction, from earth-life point of view, where you begin and end and thus where you take stock. Here you need to look at your self-concepts, how you feel about yourself deep inside when all the glamours and ego-massages and distractions are gone and there is nothing left but the bare existence of you.

Opposite you in the Northwest direction is the place of inner patterns and automatic responses. As your history formed you, so from it come your patterns and those patterns will continue doing their secret, behind-the-scenes work until you become conscious and master them. Think of any habits and addictions you may have such as smoking, alcohol, too much sugar, desperate relation-ships, over ambition, struggling to gain approval and so on. How well we succeed in self mastery directly affects our self-concepts.

THE SOUTHWEST DIRECTION
Between the South: Water - emotion - past
And the West: Earth - physical - body - present moment

is the Southwest place of the 'DREAM'.

Out of our feelings (South - at your right hand), which come from past experience and are part of the gift of water (no water - no feelings) we *'dream'* our creations into the reality of the manifest Earth-world (West – at your left hand) as co-creators with the Source (God). What we have already created is deeply influenced by our *'dreaming'*, our intent (prayer) of the past. When that *'dreaming'* is clear and focused, we influence the manifestation of our wishes in beauty, but when our *'dreaming'* is muddy and contains such things as hidden thoughts of self-sabotage, then we bring a mixed bag into being.

In spirit - and in night dreams - we can dream, build, tear down and build again, all in effortless moments, but here on earth we live in substance and we act out our dreams for 'real'. It takes time and effort to create a dream into manifestation. Here on earth we have the chance to develop, to be tested, to change, and to learn. We have the unique opportunity to experience manifesting our dreams into material reality.

Here is a simple way of calling spirit's help to manifest your dreams. Get a box, preferably a beautiful one or at least one that is beautiful to you. Put in it pictures of what you wish to call to you or objects that represent your wishes. I put the first pages of this book in my box when I wanted a publisher to show up – and a few months later he did! Put pictures, images, objects, articles, anything that encapsulates what you wish to bring to you for the good of you and the good of all. Then 'see' your wish manifest (Right now I am visualizing this book in a bookstore and being avidly read!) and let yourself accept that it will be. As Captain Picard says in Star Trek – 'Make it so'! Hold your image (I-The- Mage) of the manifest dream. Pray regularly over your box while 'seeing' your wishes manifested. As you do this with full intent, focus and certainty, so the Universe will yield your vision.

Earth - the Mother - mater - matter is our teacher. Don't divorce matter from spirit as if they are different and one is good and the other bad. There is a very strange and misguided mythology which says God lives in Heaven up above and is all good while evil lives down here on earth in hell. But hell actually means light, Hel-en is the goddess of light, and eve-il is the realm of Eve, primal woman, primal mother. Without the Mother, spirit has no individual life and no chance to directly experience choice and learn about itself and grow and develop. This is the realm we are intended to live in and our purpose is to gain mastery of living in this realm.

Now sit in the Southwest of your wheel
  Your right hand is in the South, the child, emotion, water, the past
  Your left hand is in the West of materialized reality, the physical, the body, the present moment of actualized manifestation.
  You sit in your 'dream' place and gather your inner child, your past experience, and you consciously 'dream' what you desire into your manifest physical reality. This is where visualization, conscious desiring, goal setting, ceremony, and so on come in to play.
  Opposite you is the Northeast place of choice. According to how and what you 'dream' so you will tend to make your choices.

THE NORTHWEST DIRECTION
  Between the West: Earth - body - present
  And the North: Wind - mind - thinking - future

  is the Northwest place of PATTERN AND KARMA.

Life is held in patterns - the natural Laws of the Universe and also man-made laws. Our patterns of life are habits, automatic stimulous-responses, repetitive actions. At the root of all the patterns is ultimate balance and justice, the power that maintains the balance of karma, that oversees that action brings, in the end, equivalent reaction.

All manifest life is patterned, and there are 2 important ratios. The Fibonacci ratio, named after an Italian mathematician, is the sequence of adding the last number to the one before, i.e:- 1:1:2:3:5;8:13:21:34 etc. The average of this ratio is 1.618, the so-called 'golden mean' or phi.

The second ratio is that of the diameter of a circle relative to the circumference. Known as pi, this number is 3.142..... Neither of these ratios ever resolve into whole numbers. This is important to consider - the Universe is created to exist in a state of mild imbalance. The Taoists teach that the Yin is never completely yin and the Yang is never completely yang, nothing is ever completely perfect, nothing and no one is ever completely good and nothing and no-one is ever completely bad. In my childhood I loved lupins and I remember fruitlessly searching for a perfect one. Some were perfect at the bottom but not yet open at the top and the ones that were fully open and lovely at the top were dying at the bottom. Not a single one was fully open all the way from top to bottom at the same time. There simply was no perfect lupin. It was a life lesson for me to learn, but it took me longer than childhood.

There is a very childish idea that 'God' is perfect. If so why create this extraordinary learning environment that is Planet Earth? God – Creation - is on a learning curve called Evolution! We are all part of this Great Story!

Next, sit to the Northwest on your wheel.
Now your right hand is in the West place of manifest material reality and your left in the North of intellect, knowing, believing, thinking, rationalizing and fantasizing.

You sit in the place of pattern, karma, rules and laws and you gather in the knowledge and experience of manifestation from your right hand, and the intellect and ability to work things out from your left. Material reality is held together by patterns and our mind holds information in patterns.

Opposite, you see all your history and your ancestors and all your past influences that have formed you up to now. As you sit in this place, reflect on the teaching that says 80% of all energy is patterned and habitual and 20% is available for freewill and change. That means you have only 20% of your energy to work with and alter the habitual 80%. This is highly beneficial when you have studied and worked to learn a skill, let's say to play a musical instrument. If it wasn't for the patterned 80% you would forget right away and have to learn over and over again! But when it comes to changing a no-longer-desirable habit, the same applies. You have to work and work to re-train yourself to incorporate a new habit, a new way of being. You have 20% of your available energy to put to the task of re-training the other 80% that holds the habit.

There is an interesting unwritten law in commerce that says 20% of your customers almost invariably give you 80% of your business. Back in the 60's when I was a managing director and first heard that idea I said - 'rubbish, it doesn't apply to my company, our sales are much more widely distributed'. But when we sat down and worked it out, it did. It was 20 point something per cent to 79 point something per cent!

THE NORTHEAST DIRECTION
Between the North: Air - mind - future
And the East: Fire - spirit - timeless

Is the Northeast place of CHOICE AND THE DESIGN OF LIFE.

Spirit, through the power of intellect, has chosen to manifest itself into the third dimension as the form of life we know and experience. There can be no doubt whatsoever that the Universe is an astonishingly complicated magical mystery. We live inside it as part of it and we are learning all the time how it works. We may think we are clever, finding out all the things we know, going to the Moon, landing a vehicle on Mars, creating the most amazing flying machines and travelling all over the planet, but consider for a moment the incredible power of the intelligence that set the whole thing up, created it all. Awesome just doesn't catch it. No wonder wise ancients called it GREAT MYSTERY.

CHOICE is an incredible gift of Life. Together with it comes the responsibility for the results of those choices, and this is the teaching we experience on our Great Mother Planet. The Great Mother has given us life here in a planetary spacesuit. In this life we have the right to freedom of choice. We are spirits, born from the Great Dream into an individual self-directed life where we can experience that all actions bring reactions. We are in a hall of mirrors where our self is reflected to us constantly by Life.

(If you think you are not self-directed, ask who is directing your non-self-direction?! If you are limited in what you think you can do because of, for example, civil laws, ask who is choosing to live here and obey them! Lastly, ask who chose to be born into this time and place, family and body-vehicle?)

Now sit in the Northeast of your wheel.
Sitting in this direction you draw in from your right hand knowledge and wisdom - or their concomitant bullshit and stupidity. From your left hand you connect with spirit, fire, the transpersonal and timeless realm of just being - or a fantasy world of self-importance and misuse of power over others. Opposite you is the Southwest realm of the *dream*. According to how you '*dream*' your life to be, so you affect the choices you make, and the choices you make will affect the *dreams* that you manifest. Whether what you manifest fits your idea of your dream or not, it is still what you dreamed.

There is an old saying 'Make up your mind'! The medicine wheel teaching is 'never make up your mind about anything ever again'. Use your mind for its rightful purpose of sorting, sifting and assembling knowledge, and call to your spirit for advice and guidance on making your decision.

THE CARDINAL DIRECTIONS WITH THE INFLUENCES OF THE NON-CARDINALS

The view from the South

Your left hand is in the Southwest, the *'dream'* and you right hand is in the Southeast, history, ancestry, past. Out of your past experiences and all you have inherited in your genes through your ancestry comes the material with which you *'dream'* your future life creation into manifestation.

Now what is so important and is a great trial of this life is that there can be an almightly difference between what we think we are 'dreaming' and what we actually are *'dreaming'*. This is where lack of self-worth, self-sabotage, self-hatred, guilt, shame and deep inner hidden negative beliefs can cause such disharmony between what we think we think and who we think we think we are, and what and who we really think-believe we are in our so-called subconscious mind. This is why it is so important to work hard constantly to make the subconscious conscious, to bring to consciousness and chase away the belief-viruses that are screwing up our programming. This is why so many lovely *'dreams'* bite the dust of self-sabotage.

Opposite you is the North place of mind, intellect, future. In the South you feel and this is complemented opposite by the ability to think, the one affects and interacts with the other.

The View from the West

You sit in the place of your manifested reality between your patterns and habits to your left and your 'dream of life' to the right. According to how much you have mastered your patterning - your habits and automatic stimulous-response behaviour - so you will be able to manifest your actual dreams. If you have a dream of wealth but smoke 50 cigarettes a day, the chances are your dream is going to be defeated by the cost of your habit pattern, to say nothing of its effect on your health. If you dream of taking action to live your life as you really want but your ancestors taught you self-sabotage by doing it to themselves, that will be in your patterning and will defeat your desires until you master it.

Opposite you is the East place of spirit and fire. Material reality is spirit-in-matter. To connect with your spirit-self you need to quieten your matter, hence the many tools of meditation and all such ways of stilling the mind and emotions through stilling the body.

A lot of bad mythology encourages a feeling of competition between matter and spirit and conveys the nonsense that one is good and the other bad. This is hidden in our language which says that all good is 'God'. Notice that there is just one zero difference between the words. Then look at the common word for bad - evil. Eve is primal woman, primal mother, mother earth, the matter into which spirit has chosen to incarnate. In our language, Eve-il, the workings of Eve, has been made into all that is bad. So then all that is 'spiritual' gets thought of as all that is good (God) and construed as separate from all that is matter and manifest, which gets construed as all that is bad (Evil). This is truly awesomely awful mythology and the opposite of life-affirmative. This is at the root of the non-sustainability of Western (now decadent) civilization. When people believe that the Earth is bad, the Mother is bad, material reality is bad, the feminine is bad, that woman is inferior to man and that a man's highest possibility lies in being 'spiritual' by rejecting life, rejecting woman, rejecting sexuality, rejecting his own body except for its bearest needs, or the opposite, fulfilling every greedy fantasy without respect for other life, he is conducting a war against his own source and all that sustains him. The Source - Spirit - made the choice to incarnate and a man who rejects that incredible gift is working against his own deepest nature and against his own source!

The View from the North.
As you sit in the north your right hand is in pattern and karma, rules and laws, and your left hand is in choice and design of energy. Opposite you is the South place of feeling, of emotion (energy-motion). You pull in from your right the knowledge of pattern, habit, trained aspects of self, automatic-stimulous

responses and so on, and with your left you bring in your ability to make choices. You are a co-creator of your reality so you have the ability and right (and it is encumbent on you) to choose which of those habits and patterns you wish to continue and which you choose to change.

There is a common New Age saying "You create your own reality". This has a deep flaw as it puts humans at the top of the tree of evolution rather than a part of the whole. From a shamanic point of view, a human is a part of creation and creation is not just here for humans. Our reality is created by the earth and the sun, by the plants and the animals, by the Whole Creation of which we are but one part, and which has been in existence far longer than we have. Within that awesome creation we attract events, lessons, learning, teaching and so on to ourselves like magnets, and thus all life is meaningful. But to say we humans create it all is human ego gone ballistic!

The View from the East

You sit now in the place of your Spirit, of the you that is transpersonal, that is timeless and eternal. To your right is your place of choice and to your left is your history and ancestry. Your spirit expresses itself through its body-vehicle (opposite - West) which contains your history, and yet you are free to make your choices as to your future. In the West realm of material reality is the arena in which the results of all choices are played out and experienced.

The East is where the nitty-gritty question of the Star Maiden's Circle (see section 2) comes up - 'What's the payoff?' We act out in the world but it is when we come to the place of spirit, of our essence, of our true origin, that we have to ask the most awkward questions and face up to the consequences of our actions in the material world that reflect to us how our soul is managing our Earth-Walk and whether we are developing in the directions spirit wishes or not.

In conclusion, the 8 directions show us a broader map of the powers that we are and the powers that act upon us.

PART 4 STALKING POWER

Stalking power is a major task in the shaman's life. Becoming a powerful person is about mastering life, and for that the first aspect of life we need to master is our own Self. We all tend to act like stimulous-response automatons until we gain knowledge of our inner workings and learn to override, change and master these patterns.

Here are two definitions of power from a shamanic point of view:-

1. POWER IS ANYTHING THAT CONNOT BE TAKEN AWAY FROM YOU.

Such as: – integrity, authenticity, knowledge, wisdom, experiences, memories, ability to love, self-regard, and so on.

2. THE ABILITY TO NEVER BE <u>AT THE EFFECT</u> OF ANYTHING OR ANYONE, AT ANY TIME, ANY PLACE, ANYHOW.

In other words, you may be rejected, locked up, spat on, pushed around, lied about and so on, but inside you are unwavering in your self-knowledge of who you really are and your self-regard.

PERSONAL POWER is about power over one's Self and has <u>nothing whatsoever</u> to do with political power or manipulative power to get want you want from others.

We have THREE SOURCES OF POWER:

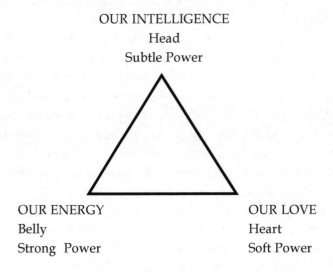

OUR INTELLIGENCE
Head
Subtle Power

OUR ENERGY
Belly
Strong Power

OUR LOVE
Heart
Soft Power

And FOUR WAYS OF EXPRESSING POWER

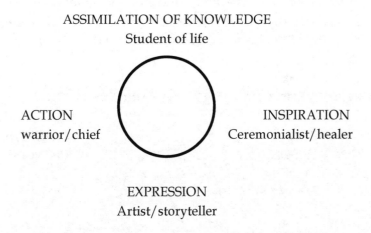

ASSIMILATION OF KNOWLEDGE
Student of life

ACTION
warrior/chief

INSPIRATION
Ceremonialist/healer

EXPRESSION
Artist/storyteller

A very interesting thought I recently heard (from writer/teacher Jose Stevens at a conference in Santa Fe) regarding the difference between predators and prey.

PREDATORS stalk opportunity, wait patiently for the moment, plan, watch, wait, and then act with will and determination.

PREY live by routines, habits, predictable repetitive patterns, patterns that can be stalked and learned by predators. These repetitive habits make prey weak and vulnerable.

How do you live? Are you predictable, habitual? Do your patterns give you away? Not just patterns of acting but patterns of thinking. Do you fall into being a recognizable 'type' or class of person, hold the same ideas, dress and present yourself as your 'type', your class? You will probably have to ask your friends to figure this out and hope they dare to tell you enough of the truth!

It is interesting to note that amongst land animals, predators generally have eyes on the front of the head while prey have them to the side. Note where your eyes are!

Our habits, routines, predictable patterns all make us weak and vulnerable. Taken one small stage further and they become our addictions and neuroses. They are the refuge of the little frightened part of us who uses routines to avoid consciousness of difficult challenges and changes.

Here is a map of our addictions, neuroses and 'pain games' called the SEVEN ARROWS. The egoic arrows show how we lose power, self esteem, self worth, self love and care. They are how Little-Ego, from his fear-place, likes to rule the roost and call the shots.

THE SEVEN 'EGOIC' or SHADOW ARROWS

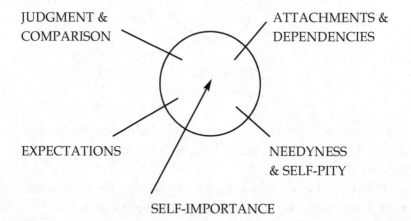

1 ATTACHMENTS - greed / desperately trying to fill the emptiness inside.

2 DEPENDENCIES - self-destructiveness. Avoidance of feelings of meaninglessness

Both attachments and dependencies come out of feelings of emptiness and meaninglessness and are little-ego's attempts to avoid and evade having to grappling with life's uncomfortable issues and challenges.

3 JUDGMENTS – Stubborness / fear of change / fear of authority hence judging others to try to avoid looking at self.

4 COMPARISONS – self-deprecation / fear of having no value as a person hence constantly comparing self with others

Judgments and comparisons are attempts to impose rigid patterns on life to avoid having to own one's fears. They are attempts to behave like predators to others which actually make oneself into prey.

5 EXPECTATIONS – impatience / self delusion.
Expectations are the mind impatiently racing ahead into delusions of future self-aggrandizement to avoid feeling and being in the actual present moment.

Also, fear of not having enough time.

6 VICTIMHOOD / SELF PITY / NEEDYNESS FOR APPROVAL.
Victimhood, needyness and self-pity are emotional indulgences of Little-Ego when he daren't face life and its challenges. Fears of being trapped by circumstances.

7 SELF-IMPORTANCE / ARROGANCE / SELF-AGGRANDIS-EMENT.
The pride that comes before the fall. Fear of being vulnerable.

How do we lose power? Let's play around with these arrows

How often do you feel you are a victim of life, the system, difficult people, rising prices, the government, 'God'? How much do you feel the need to fit in, belong, conform? What are you addicted to, fixated upon? What would you sell yourself to gain? This is the source old Biblical and horror movie expression - 'selling your soul to the devil'. The following are all ways to do this - to maintain yourself in a state of pain and powerlessness while expecting to gain some impossible advantage.

A good title for these habits is *'Pain Games'*

See if you recognise aspects of yourself (or more likely people you know) as we go through these addictions:

1. *Attachments*

Take a look and see if you might be attached to any of the following:

An image of youth and beauty, attractiveness to sexual partners? Then ageing will be a challenge .... and it comes to all of us regardless.

Celebrity status? Celebrity is ephemeral and can disappear at any time; just like fashion, it can change on a whim - and it has little to do with the actual person concerned anyway. But if you have celebrity status and believe in it, then loss of it will feel like a big rejection.

Money and the status it confers? Attachment to lots of money can make you vulnerable to life's changes in the financial arena.

2. *Dependencies.*

Drugs of all sorts such as cigarettes, alcohol, coffee, dope, pharmaceuticals; comfort makers such as gossip, compulsive TV watching, compulsive computer playing, masturbation, sugar, chocolate, junk food, compulsive adultery; co-dependent relationships with attitudes such as 'I love you, can't do without you, I hate you and can't stand being with you'.

Dependencies are a way we try to cope with inner misery, an attempt to assuage feelings of loneliness and isolation. Instead of facing what's true and getting to grips with life, we get into a self-destructive cycle. We affirm the false self who is fully defended and lives in resistance to what is happening if it doesn't suit him. In trying to keep pain at bay, we re-create it relentlessly by trying to protect ourselves from reality. In the words of John Lennon *'Life is what happens while you're busy making other plans'*.

Attachments and dependencies have similar roots - fear for security, fear of not enough, fear of being alone. They are attempts to create a false series of barriers around us to protect us from the truth. And the truth is that we are all incredibly vulnerable to life and its challenges and vissitudes and no amount of money, apparent power or status will save us from experiencing changes.

Remember Pompeii - or the crash of 1929 - or WW1, WW2, OR 9/11 or the recent devastation of numerous people's pensions, or the Asian Tsunami? Life is insecure and the only certain thing is that we all get to die sometime. And no, that is not a miserable statement, it is a simple blunt truth. The question is how we live the time we have till then. That is the crux of life - living the time we have fully, joyfully, creatively, following the feelings that bring us towards the wonderful state of bliss.

The Authentic Arrows are self awareness and self-appreciation. It is by appreciating and valuing our-self that we gain the strength to fight dependencies.

3. *Judgments.*   *"Those kind of people, 'them', I'm not like them. I mean would you dress like that? I wouldn't be seen dead in a suit like that - and with a grey tie? And brown shoes??   I mean I'm not one to make judgments but..... And her, who does she think she is? Just look at that dress for heaven's sake, talk about mini-skirt that's more like a belly skirt. Personally, I'm not judgmental at all but......."*

Put downs, fault finding, the see-saw effect of making oneself feel better by knocking others. Judgment comes out of our inner *rules and laws* because as we judge others, so we are judging ourselves. One important thing to remember with compassion - when you listen to a really judgmental person ranting forth, take a moment to consider that they them-self, through their inner dialogue, are on the receiving end of that virtually all the time!

The judgmental person attempts to become stubbornly invulnerable and in control all the time. This leads to a crushing of the libido as after all, one has to be vulnerable to make love. Instead he may enact impersonal 'bonking' sex (or masturbation - that's really 'safe' and one is fully in control!) - while remaining invulnerable and in denial of any feelings that may occur.

While attachment is what joins us to mother, judgment can often be what we get from father. If father has been inwardly destroyed and has survived by becoming heartless, he will tend to destroy his offspring by doing 'good' for them as he sees it 'should' be done. By rules and criticism he will attempt to put his children 'right', and they will end up hating him for it.

The useful side of judgment is discernment, and we all need good discernment to function well in life. To not judge does not mean to accept everything blindly, that is stupidity. It is the negative, separating energy of judging others that hurts, the rejecting of others and their dreams that is just a fragile ego struggling to prop itself up by putting others down.

Being Judgmental maintains pain, loneliness and separation. To be good at judging others, be rigid, be right, and keep a list of put-downs ready for all occasions. Remember you are special and superior. It won't make you popular but it will keep Little-Ego happy. For now, anyway.

The Authentic Arrow is self acceptance as it is through embracing this quality that the need to judge others can be released.

4. *Comparisons.*
Us and them. *Are you one of us, the in-group? Or one of them, the poor failing excluded unfortunates, the lesser mortals? Are you one of God's chosen people or just some ordinary jerk?*

Constant comparing of self with others comes from a deep fear of not being of value.

Comparison is about the pecking order on which so much

normal civilisation depends for its structure and maintenance. It is the galvanizing together into a collective group identity of 'us' and 'them'. In an ultimate sense it is about whose 'god' is the 'one true god'. Ultimately, all non-believers, all of 'them', must be driven out to maintain the purity of the in-group. Ethnic cleansing, racism, racial purity, family blood purity, colour prejudice, class distinction, religious fanatisism and all such ways of bolstering a sick ego belong here.

A person mired in the arrow of comparison will see others' achievements as a threat. Perhaps even as an attack on himself and a reinforcement of his fear of not being a person of value. This creates more sense of isolation and pulls in convoluted desires such as to attack and hurt the achiever. One way to assuage this is to self-deprecate, to criticize and put-down oneself first. (We Brits are specialists at this!)

The Authentic Arrow is self-pleasure. It is by extending self awareness, self appreciation and self acceptance into self pleasure that one can begin to let go of the needing to compare oneself and the sense of alienating competition that it generates.

Expectations.
"Never mind the present, son, look to the future. Suffer now, work hard for a pittance, and one day you'll get your reward. Follow in my footsteps, son, do as I do, believe what I say. If you don't get your reward on earth, you'll surely get it in heaven". There is a religious version of that too, especially for poor people to encourage them to be compliant and accept powerlessness. In the centre of so many impoverished communities is a rich and splendid church or cathedral. What does that tell you about where energy went, where the money has gone, where the power lies?

'Look to the future with impatience. You are here but you want to be there! Look at all the goodies you are expecting to happen, all the fantastic future moments you lust for. To be good at expectations, the secret is never to be in the present. Hope springs eternal and hope is about the future. (*By the way, are all your insurance policies up to date?*

Specially the ones that pay out after you are dead......)

The Authentic Arrow is *self-love*, and love exists only in the present. You cannot love tomorrow - you may intend to - but you can only actually love now. Love is a verb, not a noun, and calls for action in the only time that exists - now!

Victimhood / Needness for approval / self-pity.

Isn't it nice to feel liked, given regular ego massages, lots of acceptance, support, 'love', chocolate? To succeed at this arrow, all you have to do is give away your rights, your power, your opinions and become just the way others want you to be. In Jane Austen's *Pride and Prejudice,* one of the girls declares approvingly of one of the young men, *"And he holds all the right opinions too". Dress to please, speak to please, live to please, be self-denigrating, apologise readily. Be nice about everything, everyone....... please, please....... er, sorry.*

This arrow is home to the 'poor-me' person who never actually grew up and is still stuck in wounded child. Such people revel in problems, issues and all that life has done to them, and though they are likely to be extremely 'nice', can turn on a whisker and blame all and sundry for their life while rejecting any degree of self-responsibility.

There is a tendency here to alternate self-deprivation with self-indulgence and sometimes self-punishment. Anorexia and bulimia live here, as does masochism and the desire to be punished.

There is an expression of needyness that has caught many people these days and that is illness. The horrifying 'success' of Prozac, a dulling drug, is evidence of that. Have you ever been in a group of middle-aged people discussing all the pills they are on and what their doctor said and how many hospitalizations they've needed - just like a one-upmanship club?   Lack of spiritual connection leaves people floundering between the difficulties of everyday and feelings of inner emptiness. An easy way out is to be ill and therefore to be in need of special treatment - at least someone will take notice then - and after all it is highly socially acceptable to be ill. It combines 'poor me' victimhood with a sense of togetherness with other sufferers and a backwards sense of self-worth in affirming oneself as a walking set of special unique problems.

One of the perceptions that comes from having a state funded National Health Service is that doctors and their expensive drugs are thought of as 'free', though in fact through taxes they cost us a fortune, while herbal medicines and natural remedies cost the individual money to purchase but are much less costly overall. So it is appears to be almost cost-free to be really sick and to get special treatment and care, but if you are well and you pay for pre-emptive medicine to keep yourself healthy, it costs you and you get no special consideration!   Funny culture! Cockeyed back-to-front way of running things!

The Authentic Arrow is Self-Actualisation, the arrow of the Spiritual Warrior, who consciously creates and re-creates him/herself from a place of self-mastery. We cannot be responsible and needy, we cannot be a self-actualising adult and a needy child. We take command of the ship-of-self and see that we meet our own needs as far as we can and fully accept when we cannot.

7. Self-Importance.
"Life is serious. One simply cannot afford to waste time on trivial pursuits like laughing and frivolity and all this looking within, gazing at your navel. All this therapy, ceremony, shamanism, lying on the floor journeying to some spirit world is just self-indulgence. Haven't got time for that. I mean god is God and he is in his heaven fighting the devil or whatever and that's all there is to it. I've got things to do, meetings to attend, rising career, important people to see, full diary, decisions to make, no time, lots to get done, promotion in the pipeline, I'm needed, I'm important, I'm better, I'm the top man - or I will be soon... Excuse me, nip out and get me a packet of cigarettes would you, better make it a carton. And a bottle of scotch."

Self- Importance is the cream of Little-Ego's arrows and the summation of the other six. To succeed at this arrow you need to clear out any vestiges of a sense of humour and to remember you are entirely entitled to your arrogance which, after all, comes from your innate superiority!

Self-Importance includes both pomposity and its apparent opposite, shyness - the shy person can be just as self absorbed as the show-off. Self importance brings great loneliness and isolation and amounts to a denial of connection to spirit, to the earth, and to fellow humans. It is a whole house of cards stacked like armour to defend, deny, resist, keep out, hold at bay, not feel, not change, be invulnerable - like a rock. This pack of cards always tumbles eventually and the higher it has become, the bigger the crash when it does.

This is the totality of apparent power which in reality is just weakness.

The necessary Authentic Arrow is impeccability -

to learn to live as an IMPECCABLE WARRIOR.

AND TO BECOME A TRULY POWERFUL PERSON, SECURE IN ONE'S SELF.

THE 'SEVEN DEADLY SINS'

Here is another more familiar map.

1. PRIDE
2. COVETOUSNESS
3. LUST
4. ANGER
5. GLUTTONY
6. ENVY
7. SLOTH

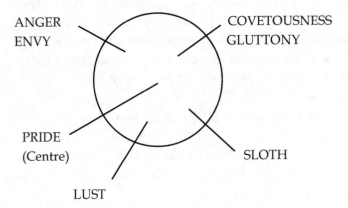

ANGER
ENVY

COVETOUSNESS
GLUTTONY

PRIDE
(Centre)

SLOTH

LUST

Let us see how the two maps compare and what we can learn from putting them together. It is good to remember that all maps are just maps, only the territory is the real thing. But it is a whole lot easier to find your way around with a map than without one.

PRIDE. From the Oxford dictionary: "Overweening opinion of one's own qualities, merits etc; arrogant bearing or conduct"

Well, that is SELF-IMPORTANCE by another name. Puffed-up, out of touch with reality, off the ground, self-aggrandizing, defensive, in denial and so on. Oh what a lovely person to meet, what a grand petty-tyrant such a person would make!

COVETOUSNESS. From the dictionary: "Eagerly desirous (of

another's property etc.), grasping, avaricious."

Hoarding, keeping, more for self... this is another way of expressing ATTACHMENT.

LUST. The dictionary says: "Sensuous appetite regarded as sinful; animal desire for sexual indulgence, lascivious, passion; passionate enjoyment of desire; have strong or excessive desire."

Well just look at the cultural emphasis in that! The linking of sexual desire and lustyness with sin as if it is automatically bad. Well, I am all in favour of 'passionate enjoyment of desire' but I do remember the religious mores of my youth, 50 odd years ago, when anything to do with sex and particularly enjoyment of it, was equated to sin and badness. Well I want to put in a good word for the joys of lusty sex, sensuous appetite and passionate enjoyment! If we do not enjoy ourselves, spirit does not get to enjoy, as after all, it is through us that spirit gets to experience manifest human life!

Now where does lust fit on the wheel? This would be EXPEC-TATION because it is about wanting, about appetite. You do not want food or sex when you have just had them, you want them before, when you are hungry! Desire is a function of expectation, wanting, so I will put it here.

ANGER. According to the dictionary: "Rage, hot displeasure, trouble; make angry, enrage."

Anger is stated as one of the *Seven Deadly Sins* but I feel there has been a translation error here. Anger itself is necessary, not wrong. The ability to express anger itself is essential and the person who cannot express anger cannot stand up for self, cannot hold boundaries, cannot put things to rights and can easily be disempowered and pushed around. Anger is a necessary tool to confront something that is wrong, bring it to rights and to return to a state of lovingness. Anger lives in the heart-centre along with love and when love is present there is no anger. But when love is denied its expression, action is called for to return things to their desired state and the rightful tool for that is anger. The word courage expresses it correctly - Coeur, the heart - and rage, the power. Power to put matters to rights.

Now anger can also be misused. Repressed anger that comes out in the wrong amount at the wrong time on the wrong person can be thoroughly destructive, and the repression of anger can cause illness too. The person who misuses their anger to ride roughshod over others or one who dumps years of frustration onto someone who makes a minor infringement are typical misusers of anger and in this way it is a 'sin'. I prefer to call this expression RESENTMENT - and it is akin to the arrow of JUDGEMENT.

I had better define 'sin' while we are at it. SIN comes from a (Hebrew/Aramaic?) word in archery which means 'missing the mark', being off centre. So a sinner is someone who misses the mark, who is off centre. That is all of us some of the time! Who is fully centred all the time? I do not know anyone, do you? That is why we are alive in a body - to learn about being centred, to find our way to balance and harmony, alignment, wisdom, lovingness.

GLUTTONY. The dictionary definition is: "Excessive eater, gormandizer; greedy, person with great appetite, voracious animal...!

Gluttony is about over eating, over consuming, taking more than your share, grasping to fill the void of yourself - and that is another way of saying DEPENDENCY.

ENVY. The dictionary says: "Grudging contemplation (of more fortunate persons)."

Looking at others and what they are, what they have. This is COMPARISON.

SLOTH. From the dictionary: "Lazyness, indolence."

Now this is an interesting additional flavour to the arrows. Sloth is lack of self care and self respect, and comes from an inner feeling of not worth it, not worth bothering with myself. This is self-pity, 'poor-me', victim consciousness and is the arrow of NEEDYNESS AND SELF-PITY.

Those are the maps of our egoic self in action, of how we lose power and become prey - so what can we do about it?

RECAPITULATION - SOUL RETRIEVAL

To heal our past – or in the words of Casteneda's don Juan and the Toltecs – to 'erase our personal history', we need to 'recapitulate' so we can bring the major events to consciousness and become able to let go of their effects.

There are myriad ways to recapitulate and here is a partial list.

The Star Maiden's Circle (See Section Two)
Inner child psychotherapy / hypnotherapy.
Shamanic soul retrieval.
Psychodrama.
Trance-Dance.
Family Constellations. (The work of Bert Hellinger)
The Toltec method of meditating in a dark box and spending time watching memories float to the surface.
Re-birthing.
Primal integration.
Regression psychotherapy.

Many of the therapies used by alternative practitioners, psycho-analysts, and some psychiatrists are forms of recapitulation. Recapitulation can also be called soul retrieval in the sense that all this work is about putting our splintered selves back together. Any therapy that helps you to heal past wounds can be included in this list.

This is not a simple task. The very part of our-self that acted in moments of trauma to protect our-self and keep our-self alive becomes, only to often, our jailer. This is where the self-saboteur is born. When the pain of trauma was too great, we were protected by the ability of our psyche to put the trauma out of consciousness. When in later life we seek to heal a trauma, our inner protector can turn on our own self and on anyone who helps us. It is still trying to protect us from unbearable pain. This can be very difficult to move through. The Star Maiden's Circle can guide us on this difficult path. (See pages 151 to 173)

One thing to watch out for is the tendency for some therapies to create a dependency by going over and over the same issue, failing to actually get to the let-go and move-on stage. This is where the shamanic understanding that we walk both the Red Road of healing and the Blue Road of spiritual awakening serves to keep us in balance and moving ahead in a constructive way.

It is important to maintain a sense of balance when looking at the map of the Seven Shadow Arrows. Of course we all have attachments, especially to loved ones. We all have dependencies too and we make judgments and we compare ourselves with others. We have hopes for the future and plans. Sometimes we are needy and feel vulnerable, and we know how easy it is to behave as less than impeccable spiritual warriors. The map is a set of guidelines. A contented life comes from keeping an eye on our-self and working to keep the areas which bring us pain to a reasonable minimum. It is gradual work, slow and steady, learning from experience, becoming conscious of when we fall into a pit and then climbing out quickly!

The way that has been common for many centuries is to castigate oneself as a sinner and blame oneself and feel very guilty. This is not a helpful way of addressing these issues. We are here on Planet Earth to learn how to be in a body and how to live a good life in the world of matter. It is much better to focus on becoming conscious of our actions and the results they produce – so gradually master more and more of our Self.

THE SEVEN ARROWS OF THE AUTHENTIC SELF

1 SELF AWARENESS
2 SELF APPRECIATION
3 SELF ACCEPTANCE
4 SELF PLEASURE
5 SELF LOVE
6 SELF ACTUALISATION
7 IMPECCABILITY

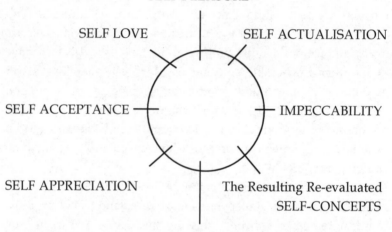

1. Self awareness. 'I am willing to look at my old mythologies, old core beliefs, old patterns and confront them. I am willing to wake up to myself, whatever it takes.'

2. Self appreciation. 'I no longer need to hold self-negating, doubting beliefs about myself. I am not a victim, I am a unique being and I am equal, no more and no less, to all other humans everywhere. I am a Child-Of-The-Universe, a son/daughter of Great Spirit. I am entitled to be here and I am needed because I am part of the Whole.'

3. Self acceptance. 'I recognise myself as a human-in-learning at the Great Cosmic School of Mother Earth. I make mistakes and I accept those mistakes and imperfections as the tools of my learning, and I hold no blame for myself and no shame in being myself'.

4. Self-pleasure. 'I no longer need to live in a state of pain and anguish. I seek a sense of pleasure and joy in everything I do. I follow my bliss.'
   (Pleasure is very often confused with indulgence. Pleasure is that which is both pleasurable and life-affirmative, indulgence can be fun but is actually life-destructive.)

5. Self-love. 'I can now love myself. In loving myself I can now love others too, and I can love Life and All-That-Is, in gratitude. Now lovingness is inside me and surrounds me and travels with me wherever I go.'

6. Warrior of the Spirit. Or 'Self-actualisation' (Abraham Maslow), 'Fully functioning person' (Carl Rogers), or 'Existential authentic person' (Jean-Paul Sartre). "I am in command of the many aspects of myself and can now dance my dreams awake and manifest them in material reality. My creative imagination sustains and creates my life into a beautiful wondrous magical experience."

7. Impeccability. 'I am always at-cause in my world. I am an Impeccable Warrior, fully responsible for myself and my life. I live and act from a place of lovingness and compassion towards all beings and all existence. I hold no regret, no shame, no blame, no guilt for being myself in my fullness. I feel my feelings but am not ruled by emotion. I act consciously in the world and I do not react unconsciously. I do not imitate others, and I do not take myself so seriously that I cannot laugh at myself and life and its wonderful absurdities and contradictions!'
   We can put these powers on the wheel as a circle of growth and development. The last place, the Southeast, brings us to appro-

priate, life affirmative, healthy self-concepts. Ultimately we move beyond self-concepts to the place of knowing there is no separate self at all, just the One Spirit expressing itself through each of us and all things.

Our human task is to learn to live as IMPECCABLE WARRIORS. A-Ho!

A personal note on this: –
All the above crystallises in our self-image – how we see, feel, believe our self to be and what we believe we are capable of. Way back in the 1960's my mother gave me a book to read by a plastic surgeon called Maxwell Maltz. He had discovered that many people's lives changed after surgery (primarily facial) as they felt they had a new and improved image. He called the work he developed from this *Psycho-Cybernetics*. I was too young and insecure to act much on this knowledge at the time but I realized later that he was absolutely right. It is how we see our-self that governs who we become and what we believe we are able to do. In another way, the movie 'The Matrix' (first one) deals with this as the hero, Neo, struggles to realize that he is a function of his beliefs - once he masters them he becomes almost limitless.

I have struggled for more than 30 years with the embedded patterns and beliefs lodged deep inside my mind and body by early programming and fear for survival. Freeing myself has proved to be a long and arduous process as one pattern dislodged makes way for yet another to call for attention. It feels endless yet I see immense progress over the years from who I was to who I am. I have also learned that the psyche can only cope with so much change at one time and that the process must proceed at a measured pace and not attempt too much too quickly or a 'fuse' may be blown. That is the fuse that can lead to depression, loss of energy, the feeling of loss of knowing what is reality, the fuse called spiritual emergency.

Let us look back now on those early years where so many patterns and beliefs get formed in our subconscious / unconscious / inner mind and where the stimulous-response automatic aspect of our-self is created.

EARLY INFLUENCES

How were you formed in your early life? What were the early
forces that moved you? The prime forces that acted upon you in
that early time were your parents, siblings and carers. You picked
up patterns that helped you survive then, many of which will be
counterproductive now.

EARLIEST YEARS:

As an infant we were all truly helpless, dependent beings. For the
first 2 years or so we lived in the 'garden' without words and
without inner dialogue, our way of expression was immediate
instinctual emotional reactions that blew through us instantly.
(Watch any young child) A child cries when it is in need and
learns very early the power of the scream and the cry to get its
needs met. Before the child can speak it learns 'I have power, I
scream and someone comes and gives me what I need'.

In the indigenous cultures a child was held constantly and fed
whenever it indicated its need. (See *Jean Liedloff - 'The Continuum
Concept'*) But in our history, nature has been interfered with by
silly theories about meal times, discipline, the cockeyed idea that
letting the child cry without support is somehow good for it, and
through such idiocies many a western child learns very early on
that it cannot trust either its instincts or its environment. So no
wonder we have so many family and school problems! One of the
best known and used parenting manuals of years ago was written
by a certain Dr Spock (not from Star Trek!), a man supposedly
knowing more than women about birthing and early upbringing...
The only mythology in history in which man gives birth is the
Middle Eastern Judao-Christian myth of the birth of Eve out of
Adam. In all the other cultural mythologies, as in life, man is
birthed out of woman!

As we grow a little older the time comes when we begin to learn
language and our parents start to teach us what is *right* and what
is *wrong*. This is the 'fall' out of the garden of instinctual knowing

and into the realm of humans who have 'eaten of the tree of knowledge of good and evil'. It takes place in our early training as we are taught to become the child they want. No longer is it enough just to react spontaneously. Now we have to think first, we have to calculate what is OK and what is not, what will get their love and what will get rejection and blame. And then we start to work out what we can get away with and what we can't, or at least what is and isn't worth it! In this process we slowly become a normalised, conditioned, acculturated, domesticated human and we learn to fit in, say the right things, do the right things, even think the right things, often quite forgetting that they aren't our own thoughts at all!

THEN LATER IN ADULT YEARS:
Here are some relationship tendencies to mull over:

In intimate partnership you will tend to re-create the kind of relationship you had with your parents, and what remains unresolved between you and your (internalised) parents will tend to come up with your partner. Put it another way, your intimate relationships in the present will serve to point you to whatever you need to heal that is left over from your past.

You 'adopt' your parents! - You will tend to copy the relationship your parents had with each other by acting out their roles with each other. This is an unconscious way of justifying them and making them 'right'. We tend to do this until we liberate our-self from our personal history.

You will tend to recreate with your partner the disapproval your parents gave you and you may well disapprove of him/her just like your parent(s) did you. Alternatively, you may overcompensate to make things terribly nice with them at whatever cost to you and your truth. Watch for a 'different' voice coming out of you. You bet your partner will notice and will let you know soon enough!

Many of us had big struggles with our parents in early years - that was pretty much 'normal' in our culture and time. Therefore a successful, smooth loving relationship can feel unfamiliar and threatening, even unexciting as if turmoil should be the order of the day. It shouldn't! WATCH in case your unconscious creates it and STOP!

Remember, at a hidden subconscious level, most people want to remain children all their lives and be told what to do, how to be, what to think, what to do, what to worship, and to be reassured they are OK and will get to 'heaven' with no worries when the end comes!

Parenting is both the most beautiful giveaway to the future of human life on earth and the most impossible job anyone can attempt. There is no way to be a perfect parent and all parents have to go through some degree of natural and healthy rejection by their offspring in teenage years so the children can separate and find themselves. Being a 'good enough parent' is quite enough and an absolutely massive achievement.

Social mores pull on parents almost more than anyone. To bring up children 'correctly' means invariably to bring them up 'normal'. That means similar to everyone else. If that is a disaster, no one will blame you because you are the same as them. (Also a disaster) But if you dare to bring up your child differently to the norm, you are likely to be castigated merrily, especially if the slightest thing goes wrong, quite irrespective of whether the end result is vastly better. Now if you are living in a crazy, unsustainable culture in which the predominant mythologies (the stories we tell ourselves which form our belief systems and the consensus world view and outlook) are false, misleading and even verging on the absurd, you have a serious problem.

And we have!

So let us take a moment and look at 'normality'?

A STRANGE THING CALLED NORMALITY

Let's take a considered look at what is considered 'normal' from a Shamanistic understanding and a western cultural point of view and make a comparison of these world views.

In the Shamanistic understanding of the cosmos, it is seen that the cosmos works according to its own natural laws. As aspects of the cosmos, it is essential for us to know the laws under which our existence operates. These laws have been obfuscated in the last thousands of years to disempower people for the purpose of political and religious domination. Under the shamanistic under-standings that follow is a summary of the essence of what I have come to understand to be the fundamental way things work, distilled from many sources, and the Western view is intended as the kind of response a fairly typical mainstream 'normal' person might make.

SHAMANISTIC UNDERSTANDING: ALL-IS-ONE.
Everything is energy. Matter is energy in 'solid' form. All is connected in a great web of life. The Creator and the Creation are One. The Creator is in Everything and Everything is in the Creator. All beings are part of the Creator and are born from spirit to matter and will die and go back into spirit. Matter, emotions, mind and spirit are different levels of one energy.

WESTERN VIEW: *I live in a separate and pretty hostile universe. 'God' is out there in somewhere called Heaven and it is up to me whether I choose to believe in Him or not. It is nonsense to say He is in everything, there are lots of foul things He can't possibly be in. The idea that He is in the fields and the trees is ridiculous and just some New Age fad for loony tree huggers. There is one life, and when I die I will go to heaven or hell according to what I deserve.*

We humans are part of life, neither superior nor inferior to other life forms. We are made of the same flesh as the animals and eat the same plants, share the air, water and everything else. We are born in the same way, we die the same way and our bodies become part of the soil to nourish future generations.
Don't be silly! God gave us dominion over the earth and everything on it. We are infinitely superior to other life which is here for us to use as we will

'REAL' LIFE IS INNER LIFE. Events happen in outer reality but our experience of them is within. The thought comes before the action. Imagination comes before 'reality'. The 'dream' becomes the manifested experience.

Real life is out there and what's out there is what is real. Things happen and we can think about them but the idea that thought precedes reality is ridiculous. Outer reality is what is real. I cannot control it by just thinking about it, I have to get out there and do things.

ULTIMATE REALITY IS TIMELESS, linear time is a function of the third dimensional mind. Within time, all things change all the time. All forms of all things are potentially transformable into all forms of all other things. As the trees breathe in, we breathe out, as we breathe out, the trees breathe in. A cow is walking grass, faeces are fertiliser, a dead body is consumed by worms and becomes soil, a rusty car becomes a chemical deposit.

Change is the constant. A shaman is someone who can touch into the timeless world to transform energy in the ordinary timebound world and thus affect 'reality', to heal and create change for the good of all.

Its been scientifically proved trees provide oxygen but everything changeable into everything else? - gimme a break! Change happens but the idea that you can 'touch into the timeless' and change reality is just a load of science fiction bunk.

THE POINT OF LIFE IS THE JOURNEY, not the destination. When we arrive, it's over! It is a co-operative venture between all manifest and non-manifest beings of Creation. We co-create it as we go along. Existence is exploring existence and we humans are front line experiencers.
The point of life is the destination. I have to get on with my life and do my best to make it and to get there. When I get there I can retire and enjoy life. Until then it's up to me to keep working towards my goals.

The first two Sacred laws of the Native American spiritual teachings are:

ALL IS BORN OF WOMAN. The feminine energy, 'Great Grandmother WAKAN', is the creative and receptive energy of the Universe. The masculine energy, 'Great Grandfather SSQUAN' is the active and conceptive energy which carries the I-mage. The feminine births and gives form, the masculine actively takes that form and creates with it.

It's a man's world, run mainly by men and God is masculine and His only son was a man. Woman may give birth but the world depends on men to run it, it has throughout history and it always will. That's what the Bible teaches and we need to take heed of that.

NOTHING MUST BE DONE TO HARM THE CHILDREN. This means all children of all races and it means the child within oneself. It also means all the children of all kingdoms of Grandmother Earth. It means don't hurt the animals - kill for food as necessary but not for sport unless someone is going to eat it. Care for the planet, the water, the air, respect the rights of all species. Shamans say we humans are intended to be caretakers of the planet. It would benefit all life for us to live in balance with this Law

Yes everything should be done to help children but animals need to be farmed for food and crops grown efficiently to create prosperity. God gave us dominion over the earth, and it's our job to take control of it and get things done.

LAWS OF ENERGY:
UNIVERSAL HARMONIC LAW: - maximum efficiency with minimum effort. (Otherwise you are out of harmony).

You know those days when nothing goes right, everything takes a long time and you just seem to get nothing done. You are out of harmony with this law. You are operating on maximum effort with minimum efficiency. Slow down, take a break, get into harmony, alignment and balance by taking time to work on the inside of yourself. When you are in harmony, things will work synchronistically with much less effort.

I am into efficiency but this sounds like an excuse for taking it easy. Hard work never hurt anyone and you have to work to get things done. As for taking time to work on the inside of yourself, well what a load of old cobblers, just another convenient excuse for idleness.

80% / 20% LAW. Energy is 80% planned and repetitive and 20% unplanned and changeable.

2x0 is the infinity sign and 8 is the infinity sign standing up. The teaching is that 80% of energy is programmed to repeat itself habitually and 20% is available to freewill, choice, accident and spontaneous happening. This means the future is impossible to fully predict and also that change within ourselves takes effort to achieve. It also means that once you have learned a skill like driving a car or typing, (as I am at this very moment) you don't forget the skill quickly. You have 20% of your energy available to train the other 80% to learn to do the things you want. 20% of your energy is your freewill and therefore old patterns will keep on trying to re-assert themselves until a sufficient amount of inner work is done to retrain the other 80%.

I am in full control of 80% of my life - or more - and I suppose possibly 20% is random or accident or something else. I don't need to train my energy and do all this so called inner-work, I just get on with things.

The above describes two very different ways of thinking, of conceiving of and attempting to understand the world we live in. The question of HOW WE THINK is vital to how we create our experience of the world. The way we are trained to think in westernized culture is to analyse and to separate and to judge and to look for answers in terms of either-or, yes or no.

And this is…….. **THE BINARY CON**

Do you believe in GOD?
You are supposed to answer yes or no

But there are two problems with that. One is what the questioner means by the term 'God' and the other is the concept of belief. If you **know** God - Spirit – Essense – Creation – Consciousness - and feel it all around, you cannot answer yes or no, that is like saying you believe or disbelieve in existence, which is absurd. Only if you postulate a separate 'God' in someplace else, not part of this world, can you answer that question as expected.

Do you believe in UFO's?
Come on - yes or no?? But I have never knowingly seen a UFO so I can't be sure and I certainly cannot dismiss the idea because there is so much evidence that many strange things exist out there. So I neither believe nor disbelieve. I am open-minded.

Do you believe in…. ?
Fill in the usual suspects and look for the Binary Con in each of them. You are supposed to be on one side or the other, open mindedness is called wooly thinking in this know-it-all age!

HOW we think affects how we make choices, how we live, how we expand or limit ourselves. If we think only in binary terms, we generate a very limited window on a vast world and cut out of view a whole host of possibilities and potentials. To expand the window we have to accept that we actually *know* only a little. We can only *KNOW* through experience and we have just so much experience. By believing all sorts of things without experience we actually shut out enormous potential knowledge. We behave like a computer - garbage in = garbage out!

And we can feel nice and safe and wise and full of information and we can talk like an expert about lots of things we've never experienced and impress people who know even less than we do and are stupid enough to accept our prejudices as real worthwhile information!

We experience two fundamental states of being. These can be

named in a number of ways:-

INCLUSIVE	-	FRAGMENTAL
CONNECTED	-	SEPARATED
COMPASSIONATE	-	FEARFUL
HEAVEN	-	HELL

These states are not opposites as one cannot exist without the other or even without the other as a point of reference. They are partners and we exist along a line between them, never arriving at the absolute extremes.

At the current time, most live way out on the fragmental side of separation, fear and hell, in a world full of competition, attempts at domination, large doses of control, manipulation and narcissistic self-importance as exemplified by the cult of celebrity. This, surely, is 'reality' in one of its most bizarre manifestations!

The strangeness of 'normality' can be seen at its strongest in the religious-scientific-materialist, which I think includes a substantial proportion of Western populations. To be a good scientific materialist one believes only in what is logical and provable – until Sunday when one goes to church and professes belief in a whole host of highly speculative and quite unprovable 'articles of faith'!

And most essentially

ONE NEVER NOTICES THE CONTRADICTION!

Neitzsche agrees with me, if a touch more verbosely!

'Even if language, here and elsewhere, will not get over its awkwardness and will continue to talk of <u>opposites where there are only degrees and many subtleties of gradation</u>: even if the invererate Tartuffery of morals, which now belongs to unconquerable "flesh and blood", infects the words even of those of us who know better —- here and there we understand it and laugh at the way in which precisely <u>science at its best seeks most to keep us in this simplified, thoroughly artificial, suitably</u>

<u>constructed and suitably falsified world</u> —- at the way in which willy-nilly, it loves error, because, being alive it loves life.

From '*Beyond good and evil*' by Frederick Neitzsche.

There is much more to this, however, and the basis of it started around 2500 years ago with ancient Greek thought versus that of the Chinese and Hindus. The Greek philosopher Democritus, known as the 'father of materialism', was able to identify the atom which he so named as it means *indivisible*. It was assumed he had found the smallest unit of matter and that the Universe was therefore created out of very small objects which could be studied scientifically and objectively from outside. It followed that through study one could discover absolute incontrovertible facts and make categorical yes/no assertions about things. This is the origin of 'Binary Con' thinking and this rigid style of thinking has come down to us as a foundation paradigm of our culture.

In China and India things were understood differently. The Chinese Taoist teaching of the dance of the Yin and the Yang where the yin is never completely yin and the yang is never completely yang suggests that we should take care before granting absolutes. Then when one looks at the dance of Shiva and Shakti as understood in the Hindu teachings we see an expression of the two primary forces of the Universe in a great flowing endless and ever-changing cosmic dance, not fixed or rigid at all.

David Ash, in his recent book – '*The New Physics of Consciousness*'- says that what has been overlooked or wrongly identified is that the energy behind reality has two primary forms, wave and spin, the one represented by Shiva – the yang masculine wave - and the other by Shakti – the yin feminine vortex. Along with other advanced quantum thinkers, he suggests that there are no particles, that no-thing is here, that reality is a wonderful weaving of energy but has no actual literal substance, no actual particles at all, just energy in forms! The wave gives us light and radiant energy while the vortex gives us energy in spin which we experience as solid matter. In the words of scientist Fritjof Capra: 'There is motion but there are, ultimately, no moving objects; there is activity, but there are no actors; there are no dancers, there is only the dance.' (From: *The Turning Point*)

This is the ancient shamanic understanding and it has been preserved, to some extent at least, by the Chinese, Indian and other cultures of the east. Not by western culture, however, where the binary, separated, fragmental concepts of life have gone hand in hand with the banishment of 'God' from here and every-here to the outer reaches of elsewhere from which 'He', already separated into masculine half only, looks down on upon us separate mortals in our separate little lives from somewhere safely separate, way, way out there, up above and far away.....

This brings me to the need to define FAITH and BELIEF.

A lot of religious people talk about faith when they actually mean belief. Faith means trust in the Universe, in Existence, in one's Inaliable Right to exist as part of this Incredible Existence, this Fantastic Vast Unfathomable Universe, this Great Mystery.

The moment one postulates a specific set of concepts as to how it is, one is not longer talking about faith but belief. To postulate a separate God-figure who is somewhere else and supposedly created the Universe separate from himself, is stepping into the realm of fantasy. It is nothing more than a Father Christmas / Santa Claus figure for adults who haven't grown up and need a 'Big-Daddy-in-the-Sky' to make them feel secure.*

Faith is about trust in existence, in the miracle of being, of existence. To have FAITH is an essential for health, hope, happiness, harmony and all such good things, and places oneself firmly within the Goodness of All Creation.

To BELIEVE in just one specific concept of God and make all other ways wrong is to separate oneself, sit in judgment and create loneliness and isolation. This is the 'Binary Con' In action.

See: 'Adam and Evil: the 'God' who hates sex, women and human bodies' by The Heyeokah Guru.

THE MEDICINE WHEEL OF PARENTS.

I learned this medicine wheel from Harley Swiftdeer in the 1980's and have appreciated its wisdom, but I have to say I have no idea if there is anything 'old' about it and I wonder if Swift extrapolated it himself. All credit to him if he did - there is nothing on earth wrong with making something up. Everything has been made up by someone sometime! To validate something just because it is old or from an exotic land far away is to negate our own creativity and validity as human beings. Medicine - soul food, wisdom, healing knowledge, knowledge of human inner workings - has always been understood by shamans as something that 'lives' and therefore changes and grows according to the changing needs and growing knowledge of the people. If it stays stuck and becomes a belief system and dogma, then it becomes fossilised and stuck - and we see enough of that in religion. Accordingly, I have somewhat re-worked the wheel I was originally taught in the light of my years as a practitioner.

Parents are placed on the non-cardinal points because they are movers of energy. (If you don't agree, just pay them a visit!)

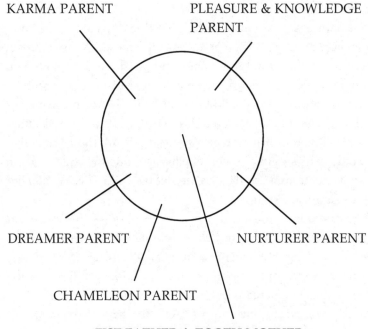

KARMA PARENT   PLEASURE & KNOWLEDGE
PARENT

DREAMER PARENT   NURTURER PARENT

CHAMELEON PARENT

FIST FATHER & TOOTH MOTHER
'GRAND' MOTHER/FATHER PARENT

Parenting is an ongoing experience over a great many years and it is a mutual relationship with the child. What we are looking at here is only a tiny fraction of a vast undertaking and only a very generalized overview. This book is primarily concerned with healing the self in adult life so it is in that context that we will look at the leftover effect of archetypal styles of parenting.

Parenting is also a developing relationship over time and what works at one stage does not necessarily work at another. Some parents may be very good at one stage but come unstuck at the next. For example, a parent who is a natural nurturer and loves to look after a little child and see that it is well cared for may be unable to give it the freedom to develop as it begins to grow towards autonomy. The wheel is an indicator of the stages of development.

From birth a parent needs to be a NURTURER (SE) and to constantly give the child its food, change its nappies and see that its needs are met.

It is natural for parents to have a DREAM (SW) for their child for his/her future. This is great if it fits with the child's own dream but not if the child's natural talents and proclivities are different, as is often the case. Then it becomes important for the parents to allow and encourage the child to develop his/her own dream.

There comes a time when the child needs to learn responsibility and that all action brings reaction, i.e. KARMA (NW), and that autonomy comes with a price. As parents guide the child to learn this by stepping back, so they further let the child develop his/her own dream for the future.

Some time later the child needs to develop his/her own will and become the designer and choreographer of his/her own life, hopefully seeking PLEASURE AND KNOWLEDGE (NE) though the guidance and support of the parents will likely still be needed to do this in a good, creative and healthy way.

I will put a word in here for PLEASURE! (Knowledge too).

The opposite of pleasure is misery. Which do you prefer? Which would you like your child to experience? Pleasure is often confused with indulgence but it is not the same at all. Pleasure makes the heart sing, brings a sense of joy and freedom, makes the body feel good and full of health, draws one into a state of lovingness, draws out creativity, brings out the best in us and brings a sense of togetherness and oneness, in tune with the Universe.

Pleasure leaves us feeling healthy, energized, peaceful and good inside.

Indulgence may well be fun but is likely to make us ill, is greedy and needy, is about 'more for me', overeating for the body, selfish propping up of Little-Ego at the expense of others, the negative arrows of judgment and comparison. Indulgence leaves us feeling sick in one way or another and with a sense of self-disgust.

So I recommend PLEASURE! - HEARTILY!

Here is an overview of archetypal parents of the four directions.

When reading, remember the stages and bear in mind that your parents may well have been brilliant at one stage and had difficulty at another. This can help you clarify anything you need to work through in your personal history, any old baggage from childhood that you may be carrying so that you can let yourself bring to the surface anything repressed and see more clearly what is acting within you and creating reactions that may be different to the ones you consciously desire.

SOUTHEAST: *NURTURER PARENT*

(Southeast - Our self concepts, history, ancestry, the lineage we come from.)

Authentic mirror:

These are parents who are socially-acceptable and in the mainstream. They are therefore like their culture and in a strong and healthy culture they will be just that, but in a sick culture they will tend to exhibit the typical problems of the culture itself. Their major purpose in life is raising and nurturing children and they identify strongly with that. They love their children and seek the best for them.

Unfortunately, however, Western socially acceptable parents are likely to ridicule their childrens' inner world of fairies, nature spirits and invisible (to most adults) friends until the children learn that they have to give it up. They are likely to promote hard work and getting on with it - or the reverse of that. They will teach of a separated world and a separate masculine God that one has to fear rather than love, and believe in but not dare to know. They will do their best to equip their children to live in the world that they experience but no more.

Egoic mirror:

These are the parents who live for their children and give all to their children whether the children want it or not. Their children can do no wrong (or right) so they grow up self-important and undisciplined or smothered into submission. The parents concept of self comes from their children and they feel their main life purpose is their children. Thus they tend to be over-protective and over-involved in their children's lives - in essesse, over-nurturing. When the kids grow up and leave, their world will tend to collapse.

They mean to teach good things but tend to end up achieving the opposite effect.

Example: Brie in Desperate Housewives.

'Don't make a fuss, people will hear.'

'You must grow up into the right sort of person, dear. Always consider what other people will think of you before you do anything.

'What will people think of us when they see you going about doing that? / looking like that?? / behaving like that???

'Mother's here to support you. Daddy's here paying for you.....you must be feeling so GRATEFUL. Never say we don't look after you,dear, because -

- we do, we do, we do, WE DO IT ALL FOR YOU'!

'Of course we KNOW you will look after us when we are old....'

'You COULD have phoned, you know you could...'

Child's Learned Mythology: *I will only be nurtured and accepted in life if I am the way other people want me to be. It is not OK to be myself as my self is not worthy so they must be right to smother and control me. I don't even know what my own feelings are so I must check up at all times to find out what I should be feeling in case they ask me. I must become what they want if I am to survive and to get any love. I must be grateful - very VERY grateful.*

2. SOUTHWEST - *DREAMER PARENT*
(Southwest - Our 'dream' of life, the reflections of life experience.)

Authentic mirror:
These parents provide well for their children and while they have dreams for their children, they are willing to listen and adapt to the child's desires. They help the child manifest his/her own dream

and their prime desire is for their child to turn out well and happy. They have good dreams - intentions - for their childrens' future.

Sometimes these parents have set aside their own dream in order to parent (Or they have never been aware of or dared to claim their own dream). They work hard to make their children the best and to give them all the best opportunities as they see fit.

Egoic mirror:
They want their children to live up to their great expectations, live out their dreams – 'follow in Daddy's/Mummy's footsteps' – or fulfill their unfulfilled dreams, actualise what they could not do, or chose not to do. Anything outside the way they see life is likely to be taboo.

They are likely to manipulate their children to make them do it their way. They demand approval from their children and are likely to threaten abandonment if they don't get it.

Examples: Neela in ER, parents of many tennis stars, and many child pop stars and actors.

> *'I sacrificed it all for you and what do you care, look at you, lazy, idle and good for nothing.'*
>
> *'We had a great future mapped out for you and look what you've turned into.'*
>
> *'You don't appreciate all we do for you, you're selfish and you give nothing back.*
>
> *'How could you do this to me, if only you had just followed my advice.*
>
> *'If you carry on like this we simply won't be able to look after you...'*
>
> *'Of course you DIDN'T BOTHER to phone, did you?'*

These parents want their children to actualise their (the parents) *dream* - but also some don't want children to be better than them and so actually give a double message. The children lose their creativity except for what the parents want them to do and the extent they feel allowed to do it.

Child's learned mythology:- *'I must live up to THEIR EXPECTA-TIONS and succeed in what they want me to in order to get any love and acceptance. I am not entitled to live my own dreams, I dare not even think about it, I am just a commodity with no value as myself.'*

3. NORTHWEST: *KARMA PARENT*
(Northwest - the place of karma, of pattern, of rules and laws, of action brings reaction.)

Authentic mirror:
These are parents who speak what they know. They teach children responsibility for their own individuality and autonomy, to accept and learn from their own karma, the life lessons they are here to learn. They teach the child honour, integrity, to giveaway and to 'Walk the Talk'.

When they are old enough, they let the children make their own mistakes and help them to learn from them. Rather than over protect the child, they might let the child mess up and then ask - 'What did you learn?'

They can appear to be unloving, but actually give a lot of unconditional love.

Egoic mirror:
Masters of guilt, blame, shame and rules. They are convinced they know the right way - all the rules for what is right and how things should be.

They can become abusive in the expression of their strongly held convictions, their rigid patterns and dogmas. They may tend towards fundamentalist attitudes.

They may let child mess up and then laugh and say 'Haha I told you so'. The children are often crushed into submission or driven to spectacular rebellion.

Examples: Some stiff upper lip military and religious families where the dogma and rules are all. Some wealthy upper-class families where children are brought up by nannies who give them more time, love and care than the parents. The boarding schools that these (dis)advantaged children are sent to / abandoned at.

> *'Father's (mother's) right, look WHAT A MESS you've made on your own. I always knew you would. Next time, do it the way you are told.....'*
>
> *'This time you are going to do WHAT I TELL YOU and you are not going to argue, do you hear??'*
>
> *'Oh, you cannot possibly be feeling that, don't be silly dear, you MUST be feeling like this!'*
>
> *'I told you what to do but you DIDN'T LISTEN did you, just look what a mess you've created.'*
>
> *'What d'you mean you're not going to church. You ARE!'*
>
> *'You SHOULD have phoned......'*

Child's learned mythology: *'I must ask before doing anything myself, be sure it will be seen as acceptable and right, and show no opinions of my own until I have checked up that they are the 'right' opinions that I may be permitted to hold. I am ashamed to be me. I dare not be creative or express anything of myself. I can speak out only so long as I say what they want me to.*

4. Northeast. *PLEASURE AND KNOWLEDGE PARENT*
(Northeast - the place of choice, of design of energy.)

Authentic mirror:
Parents who seek their own life of pleasure and knowledge as their top priority, who follow their own careers and grow and develop themselves. They assume their children want this too.

They give their children a lot of support and freedom to make their own choices and to develop themselves, and they love it when the children choose to join in parents' activities and pleasure, but support the children in whatever path they choose for themselves.

Egoic mirror:
Parents who tend towards selfishness and permissiveness. They cannot be bothered, their self focus is more important. They fail to set proper rules and boundaries for the children who consequently flounder and struggle to find their way without proper guidance. They may feed emotionally off the children.

The children can come to resent the parents for not spending time with them, not caring. In a futile attempt to gain love they can become copies of their parents and even become the parent, trying hard to create some sort of family stability. Sometimes, in an attempt to show anger and blame, they become diametrically the opposite of the parents.

Over the top example:- Edina and Saffy in AbFab.
Pot smoking, laid back parent, into own sexuality, perhaps open marriage. The child ends up trying to hold the family together.

Also Susan (and her daughter) in Desperate Housewives.

> *'Run along, dear, I've got IMPORTANT things to do'*
> *'Entertain yourself, for heaven's sake, put the telly on or something.'*
> *'Run along, dear, Mummy's busy, your 'UNCLE'S' coming round soon and you need to be out of the way'.*

And when things go wrong…

> *'You can't leave me now, Daddy needs your support. DARLING…..'*
> *'Mummy just can't cope, get me a cup of tea, DARLING…..'*
> *'You didn't phone? You just left me alone and never thought of me?'*

Child learned mythology: *'I am unloved and nobody cares for me, it is all chaos and I don't know what to do. I must be worthless. I haven't got any real parents because I am not worth it, they just use me like a convenience, they don't love me at all.'*

5. CENTRE: *GRAND MOTHER / GRAND FATHER*
FIST FATHER / TOOTH MOTHER

Egoic mirror:
Abusive parents. The father is a 'penis with knives', The mother is a 'vagina with teeth'!

They are often child victims of abusive parents themselves.

Fist father is violently explosive, (eg: The father in the New Zealand movie 'Once were warriors') and often a drunk. Punches with fist and penis.

Tooth Mother has imploded her violence and so her mothering is poisoned with suppressed rage. Child abusers and destroyers.

'You are to blame for how I am'. 'If it wasn't for you.........'

Child's learned mythology. *'I am totally powerless, absolutely worthless, just a piece of shit. I have no rights of my own and don't really exist. There is no God and if there is He won't have any time for the likes of me.'*

Later as an adolescent or adult: *'I show my power by brutality and abuse. I can show them I have power, just look who's boss now.'*

Authentic mirror:
'GRAND' MOTHER & 'GRAND' FATHER enlightened parents who live in their Centre and in their Truth and parent with light and love, infinite patience and compassion.

Parents who have truly 'erased their own personal history' and so have moved beyond worldly ambitions and who 'giveaway' to their children with unconditional love. *(A nice idea which may come about one day as the human race evolves!)*

Now there is one additional parent style I want to add to this wheel and that is the

6. CHAMELEON PARENT – who niftily moves around all parts of the wheel!

Authentic mirror:
Parents who lovingly nurture their child and grow with his/her needs as the years go by. In the early years they are good nurturers and see the child's needs are met. As the child grows they listen and support the child in its natural abilities and hear and encourage its unfolding 'dream'. When the child needs to learn responsibility they guide the child to learn and step back, giving room to grow. Later on when the child is ready to become the choreographer of her own life, and they support and encourage this while holding a secure but in no way stifling space. The results of such upbringing are likely to be excellent but the person may well be challenged by other life circumstances. (I say this because all the people I have known who have expressed great joy about their childhood and upbringing have then had giant challenges to cope with from other directions. It seems life will take us to the crux one way or another!)

Egoic mirror:
The parent who is on the wrong side at every turn. This was described to me graphically by a friend about her own parents.

SE: Early childhood to about 7. The children can do no right so they grow up either smothered into submission or else are so badly nurtured that they try to nurture the parents. The parents are over-protective and over-involved or unprotective and unable to nurture.

SW: Later childhood around 7-14 years. The parents want their children to live up to their great expectations, live out their unful-filled dreams, actualize what they could not do, or chose not to do. Anything outside the way they see life is simply taboo.

NW: Teenage years. The parents here are masters of guilt, shame, blame and rules. The emerging adolescent doesn't have a chance to emerge with these parents. They often tend towards military-fundamentalist attitudes. The children are crushed into submission and their sexuality is denied and rejected.

NE: Early adulthood. By this stage the parents cannot be bothered anymore. They have 'given up' on the children. In a futile attempt to gain love the young adults can become copies of their parents and even become the parent, trying hard to make some sort of family stability. Sometimes in an attempt to show anger and blame, they become diametrically the opposite of the parents and act out – 'give up' on the parents (though holding deep resentment).

YOUR PARENTS

It is a good exercise to see where your own parents fit into the above wheel and at what stages they significantly influenced your upbringing, positively or negatively. If you are a parent yourself, it is also very worthwhile to see where you feel you fit. To erase (the effects of) our personal history we need to know as much about our past as we can. Your parents cannot help being a very big influence on you. After all, your physical being came-to-be out of them. So the more you can do to identify their soul essence, the drives of their lives, their strengths and weaknesses, the more knowledge you will have about yourself.

I have focused largely on the challenges embodied by parents and growing up, but in every challenge, every so called 'negative' experience, there is also a gift. We grow and develop through challenge. Imagine growing up in a functional family with nothing to rebel against, nothing to push you to want to change, nothing to improve upon! Nothing to push you to become an effective and power-full person.

I remember Robert Bly, the American poet, joking at a gathering some years ago that the percentage of dysfunctional families in the USA is 102%. I responded that here in the UK we are better off because it is only 101%!

A VALUABLE LESSON IN PRESENT TIME.

Parents can present a very valuable lesson to a Warrior on the Path. When you feel you have got yourself to a place of some personal power, pay your parents a visit. Monitor your emotional self as you get to the area, the town, their street, the gate, the front door, into their house, meeting them.....

Be very aware of what goes on <u>inside</u> you, remember that the you they think they know is not the you that stands there before them. Be compassionate, but solid in yourself. Watch for the old games to be played out, be prepared to side step, be careful not to fall into victim or blamer or whatever your old defence method used to be. You are not there to teach them or to show them how good you are, or that you are a warrior. The act of trying to do so merely shows them you aren't. You are there to hold your own in a way of beauty so that any daggers pass you by, any dumps are politely rejected, any old patterns of theirs do not push you into old patterns of yours. They will only find you a warrior if you really are, and they are unlikely to realize it until much later if at all - and if you truly are a warrior, it will not matter to you whether they do or do not (though it will obviously be much nicer if they do). They may become angry, even reject you. If the price of further relationship with them is for you to give in and revert to old unhealthy patterns, you need to reject it. Politely, but firmly. Time can heal, but capitulation never does.

How you survive this test will tell you a lot about how far you really are along your path. Parents are the greatest of teachers!

LOVE THEM BUT NOT THEIR BEHAVIOUR.

In my practice I find many people struggling to love parents who have, and often continue, to treat them badly. To love your parents is natural and biological. Without our parents we do not exist in this human form. We owe our very lives to them. But that is no good reason to love their behaviour when it does not warrant it. We can love the essence of the person but we can simultaneously hate and revile their behaviour.

When a person tries to love an abusive parent's behaviour, the only way they can do that is to negate and abuse them-self. This makes the parent 'right' and therefore 'lovable'. But this is quite literally soul destroying. As a child, we may have had to put up with abuse and accept it in order to survive, and we all have an innate early programme to love our carers irrespective of what they do, and to blame ourself when they get it wrong. But as an adult it is our job to override such childhood programmes and get conscious of what is actually true.

As the old saying goes, it is the truth that sets us free.

PERSONAL MYTHOLOGIES – AND THE 'GODS' OF CHILDHOOD.

An infant is a truly helpless, dependent being. At the age of 2 or 3 or so we begin to develop language and understand the concepts of right and wrong and we think we are being taught by gods - primarily mother-god and father-god - and there is a problem here because gods can do no wrong. This is means that when parents fail to be perfect, the child blames itself and can get into enormous inner turmoil through which its natural self-love can be severely dented. There is a biological programme at work in every child to ensure that it bonds with the givers of life, its nurturers, and anything contrary done by those who are responsible brings up fear of annihilation and death - and there is no stronger motivating force. If we are abused, we tend to love the abuser and assume the abuse must be all-our-own-fault and for-our-own-good.

Core beliefs start very early and subliminally. Little girl is safe with mother and this fierce threatening dark man keeps coming and upsetting the idyll, and mother placates him each time. Message - men are the bosses and are threatening and women must give in to them for security.

Little boy with mother, safe and secure, and Daddy comes home with parcels, supplies, presents at Christmas, - and goes out again - and seems to only be at home when he is bringing things. Message - men are providers but they don't really belong at home. These are very mild examples of the formulation of core beliefs. These learned 'myths' tend to rule us until we bring them to the light where we have the power of change.

I have used an exercise with groups over many years. I ask everyone to share what has been their primary innermost negative self-negating myth/belief. While they speak them out, I write them on a board. What results from this is a kind of cultural melange of the inner pain of our time. The underlying myths are these: *'I'm not good enough; I'm unworthy; I'm unlovable'*. They are so common as to be cultural rather than personal. Religion taught our ancestors for centuries that only one man (and no woman) was ever good enough and the rest of us are miserable unworthy sinners, so it is no wonder we habitually think ill of ourselves!

Here is a selection of them from many groups over about 10 years.

> *I am not good enough, so I have to earn love*
> *I feel I must contribute to justify my presence.*
> *I don't deserve so I feel guilty when I receive.*
> *If I show who I really am, I will be abandoned and rejected*
> *I want your approval and the only way I can get it is to hide my true self.*
> *I am afraid to take my power because others will reject me if I do.*
> *I deal with other people's problems because mine are not worth dealing with.*
> *If I become independent and strong, no one will love me anymore.*
> *I can't get what I want because it's not fair to others if I do.*
> *By not letting myself know what I want, I don't run the risk of not getting it.*
> *I can't change anything, decisions are made above me.*
> *I am more spiritually evolved so you won't understand me.*
> *What the hell have I got to do for you to notice me?*
> *At least I can be bloody good at being wrong.*

When a group has completed this exercise, I like to read them a list from a previous group to point up the similarities and show that what anyone might have thought was their own original negative myth is merely a regurgitation of many others. We are all parts of one culture and the problems belong to everyone.

PUBERTY RITES – LACK OF......

One of the greatest omissions in today's world is puberty rites. The ceremonial acceptance by society of the natural – and inevitable – change from child to young adult, becoming a sexual being, the necessary change of status, and the breaking of the mother-child bond (most vital) and the father-child bond (vital though less so). The dire result of this lack is that the parent-child bonds are rarely broken and reek havoc with many people well into adult lives and leave parental relationships unnecessarily difficult for many adults.

Much need for psychotherapy comes from this dire omission to the acknowledged stages of growing up and a renewal of effective puberty rites would avoid a great deal of unhappiness and would ease relationships between very many parents and their adult children.

THE ROLE OF BETRAYAL, ABANDONMENT AND DISOBE-DIENCE IN GROWING UP

However wonderful and good intentioned our parents may have been, we all quite naturally grow up with wounding from childhood. Abandonment and betrayal are a normal part of our early learning but become traumas unless they take place with support, understanding and awareness. For example, many are taught of the figure of 'Father Christmas/Santa Claus', who delivers presents every Christmas, and there comes a time to find out it is Father and Mother, not some polar big daddy. If a child finds out by ridicule and demeaning, a piece of the imagination may shut down, but with love and care nothing need be lost.

Betrayal teaches us to rely on our self. It teaches us that life is not a nice neat fairy story where someone else will come and make everything right. It also teaches that one needs awareness and self-care to survive and thrive. Abandonment teaches us that we ultimately have to stand on our own two feet. Disobedience brings personal power, without which one is just a 'yes' person, unable to make and take responsibility for one's own choices.

Many of us take deep wounds into adulthood because our culture has lost the Rites of Passage of Puberty. Ask yourself now, at 11, 12 or 13 or so – was I guided into my new role as a teenager, into the changes in relationship with my parents and my community? Was I taught of the changes in my body, of the new parts growing in and on me? Of their purpose and how to use this new and powerful energy that my body was manifesting? Of the beauty and sensitivity that comes with bleeding, of the glorious power of erection and ejaculation? Of how new life can now be created through me?

For many ancient cultures, puberty was a time of ceremony and ritual to help and guide separation from childhood life, from the bonds to mother and father, and from dependence on nurturers and providers. It marked the beginning of responsibility for a share in the providing for family and tribe. Often a new name was taken to ceremonially mark the attainment of new status in the community, and one moved into a different place of residence.

I recently heard a story which illustrates cultural differences.

The Dalai Lama was talking at a conference of American psychologists and psychotherapists and he asked them what was the main reason people came to them for help. 'Lack of self-esteem,' was the consensus response. The Dalai Lama looked puzzled. 'What's that?' he asked.

The concept was foreign to him. Lack of self-esteem as a life issue did not exist in his culture in the same way as it does in ours.

In a culture of multi-generational families, one is unlikely to experience loneliness and self-doubt to the same degree as in the nuclear family or single parent household. Not that multi-generational families don't have their own problems, but it is important to understand that they are different.

Western culture is like a giant experiment in extreme separateness, isolation, division, loneliness, competition and individuality. In multi-generational societies a person experienced much more 'we' than 'I' -more a sense of tribe or village collective consciousness. Perhaps from a Cosmic point of view, that is the essence of the current experiment.

CONSCIOUSNESS IS CHOOSING TO EXPERIENCE ITSELF IN MAXIMUM INDIVIDUATION AND SEPARATION.

We cannot go further into isolation than one parent families unless children are brought up in institutions while everyone else lives alone. Contrast that with this: *About 20 years ago a friend of mine was visiting Grandfather Wallace Black of the Lakota Sioux in Denver, Colorado. While she was staying there, a nephew of his had a motorcycle accident and the whole extended family trouped off to the hospital. While they were waiting for the boy to come out of his operation, a nurse came in and asked 'Who is the mother of this boy?' Four women put up their hands.*

In a multi-generational society, a child grows up surrounded by carers, guides, healers, 'doctors of the soul'. Soul doctoring (therapeia of the psyche) is done in the natural course of life by such figures as Granny, Grandpa, Auntie, Wise Elder, shaman, old Friend of the family. Far enough back in time, it was the same for our ancestors.

Today the profession of psychotherapy is a response to the needs of people for whom society has broken down into small units, and for whom the ethic of competition and separation has largely defeated the ethic of co-operation and community. It is doubt of one's personal worth that is the stimulus for the competition that keeps us feeling separated.

FORGIVENESS CANNOT BE 'DONE'

Now this is a wonderful thing to do, to forgive one's parents and everyone else who 'trespassed against you'. However it is not a simple matter and is fraught with hidden problems.

From time to time I have heard some New Age guru-ish wannabee saying 'of course I have forgiven my parents long ago' (and look how superior I am) and such kind of things. I instinctively look at their body language and subtle signals and invariably I see something else, such as Little-Ego showing-off what a good 'evolved' person they are. Forgiveness has become the 'right thing to do', very PC. If it is the adult doing the forgiveness without the full blessing of the inner child, then it is just an exercise in egoism. Only when the inner child feels true forgiveness can it be real and only then can the energy be truly released.

Personally, I feel that forgiveness is not something any of us can actually DO. Forgiveness is something that follows the working out of issues and may require letting the inner child blame, rage, cry and what ever else feels appropriate until such time as the well of pain is emptied. This needs to take place in a workshop situation or with a practitioner. (Remember, the person you hold issue with in your past is the one in your memory, not the person who exists now.) Then a natural and fully felt deep release occurs within and we will recognize that as the feeling of forgiveness.

SECTION TWO - TOOLS FOR
TRANSFORMATION

THE STAR MAIDEN'S CIRCLE
THE WHEEL OF OUR LIFE PROCESS

ESSENTIAL POWERS OF THE STAR MAIDEN'S CIRCLE

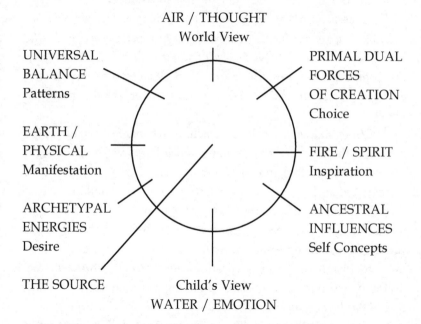

The Star Maiden's Circle is a profound tool for understanding the psyche. It is our human process in a circle. By facing each direction we gain illumination and understanding of life issues and compassion for ourself in our life struggles.

Take a look at yourself for a moment. What brought you to a path of self healing? Did you reach a point of despair? Did life take you deep into yourself and force you to ask difficult questions about your existence, your worth, your relationships to other people, to the planet, the point of it all? Rarely does anyone step onto a path to seek the Light without an experience in the Dark. For myself it was periods of deep despair and loneliness that propelled me to find something worthwhile in life if I was to continue.

Medicine wheels have been used for teaching about the cosmos since antiquity. The ancients saw their world in terms of circles and cycles and time as circular rather than linear. Medicine wheels teach of the workings of the cosmos, of the natural order, of the human's place in the natural order and of the purpose of life. They show the powers that hold the Universe in balance.

"The Medicine Wheels teach us that life is not a philosophical question . Life is our human reality, truth, fact and teacher, no matter how bitter or sweet. The Wheels teach that Life is not a religion. Rather, Life is the perfect opportunity to Learn and Grow by first questioning - asking who each human is." (Hyemeyohsts Storm - Lightningbolt p202)

The Star Maiden's Circle is a teaching wheel of the shadow, the dark and the light of being human, and it helps us to gain insight to ourselves, and thus into all humanity. The Circle of Egoic Self or 'Circle of Foxes', shows how we can chase our own tail and create a mire of our own making. The Circle of our Authentic Self or 'Dance of Coyotes' - teaches us how to seize the chance to shift our consciousness, take responsibility for our predicament, and change our circumstances. This is the path of the hero/ine who walks the mythological hero's journey, challenging demons, fighting 'dark forces' and conquering for the good of all at whatever risk to themselves. This journey is like a spiral and we walk it many times in the span of our life. When we learn the lesson offered, the challenges change next time around, but when we don't, they return - often upgraded in a more acute and painful way.

A FEW WORDS ABOUT LIGHT, DARK AND SHADOW

It is so important to understand that light is not better than dark, it is simply the opposite. Without opposites we have no definition, no difference, no polarity, no nothing! A *white-out* on a ski slope is an incredible experience of no opposites and it is seriously scary as there is no definition of anything. A white-out happens when it snows heavily and you can only see white all around you and nothing else, no horizon, no ground, no sky, no definition of any kind. Without anything to tell you of the horizon, of where you are, of which way up you are, of what is in front or behind - indeed if anything is out there at all, it is almost impossible to stand up never mind go anywhere. I speak from frightening personal experience!

We can only know anything in this realm though opposites, the manifest world is a realm of duality. We can only know light in terms of dark so how can one be better than the other? Without the polarity of both light and dark there can be no life and no challenges, no hero/ines, no illumination, no growth, no development, no change, no story, no life. Our whole *earth-walk* is set up between the two. Without duality, without adversity, we cannot grow, achieve, win, gain - and therefore learn. We cannot defeat a tyrant is there isn't one around!

Wishing that life was easy, that all was light and the dark was banished to the nether regions, that everybody was 'nice' and no one had any personality problems - well that's the same as wishing no one had a personality! It is naïve nonsense! Maturity means to bless your challengers and challenges because without them you wouldn't be alive, because you are here to grow and develop yourself, to develop your potential, to mature yourself. The challenges give you the stuff to work with for your own development.

The Native American word 'OMITAQUAYE OYASIN' means 'For all my relations'. It is traditional to say this when entering a sweat lodge and at other sacred moments. It means 'I do this not just for myself but for all I am related to'. And who is that? Its my blood relatives; it is all my human brothers and sisters; it is my animal kin, plant kin, rock kin; it is the whole planet herself. I am related to all that exists. While I am out of balance, depressed, angry, violent, I am a force for imbalance; for anti-life, (Note: live backwards spells 'evil') and I am in need of healing. As I heal and harmonise myself, I become a force for balance and for the healing of others.....

ALL PERSONAL INNER HEALING WORK IS DONE FOR THE
GOOD OF ALL BEINGS

The name Star Maiden's Circle comes from STAR - pure light of
awareness; MAIDEN - virginal, fresh; CIRCLE - the place where
two principles meet.

POINTS OF VIEW
The directions of the Star Maiden's Circle are points of view. When
we see clearly we can understand the meanings but when in
shadow or half light and we cannot see properly, we can get
fixated, addicted and confused.

Here is a diagram of the wheel more specifically related to the
human condition. You can lay this one on top of the previous one.

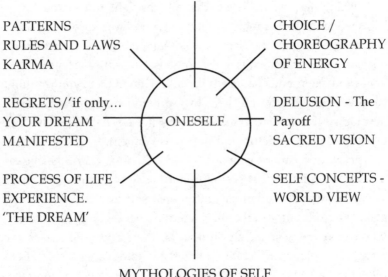

PHILOSOPHY AND BELIEF
Instinctual knowing

PATTERNS
RULES AND LAWS
KARMA

CHOICE /
CHOREOGRAPHY
OF ENERGY

REGRETS/'if only...
YOUR DREAM ———— ONESELF ——— Payoff
MANIFESTED

DELUSION - The
Payoff
SACRED VISION

PROCESS OF LIFE
EXPERIENCE.
'THE DREAM'

SELF CONCEPTS -
WORLD VIEW

MYTHOLOGIES OF SELF
The stories we tell ourselves

SOUTH:
The first direction we face is the South, the realm of water and

emotion, the place of the past and of the wounding of early life. Facing South we look at our mythologies, the stories we tell ourselves of who we think we are, the deeply held beliefs about ourselves.

The authentic-self aspect of this is our self-awareness and self confidence - our belief in our own inner worth and beauty - and is supported by all the positive, life-affirmative experiences of our past. The egoic aspects of this direction are the stories we tell ourselves of worthlessness and unlovability, the ways we sabotage ourselves, addictions we succumb to, the buried 'demons' - traumas that cause unconscious reactions in us and bring havoc to our lives.   The egoic aspects emanate mainly from negative childhood and adolescent experiences that fester within, bringing misery and unhappiness and even physical illness until such time as we shine the light of consciousness on our inner self to clear the effects of these memories, to 'erase personal history'.

SOUTHWEST:

Next we face the Southwest direction, which is the world of the 'dream', meaning how we 'see' and frame our experience of the outer world inside ourselves, how we process life's experiences and therefore how we affect the very creation of our life. For example, all those seeming happenings which 'prove' our egoic mythology of self to be 'right'. The person who says 'Oh that always happens to me, if there is shit flying around it's always my head it drops on'. Or the bad day when you got out of the 'wrong side of bed', and everything that could seems to go wrong. The Universe is very obliging! Whatever we believe, if we believe it strongly enough, the Universe will make it so. Here are some quotes from people who know the power of the 'dream'.

'The world is as you dream it'.

Numi, Equadorian shaman

'A man's life is what his thoughts make of it'.

Marcus Aurelius

"you become what you think about".

Earl Nightingale

'As a man thinketh in his heart so is he'.

Proverbs 23.

'We are what we think, all that arises with our thoughts'.

Buddha

'With our thoughts we make the world'.

Buddha

Whether you think you can, or whether you think you can't, You're right!'

Henry Ford

'The ancestor of every action is a thought'.

Emerson

Sow a thought, reap an action
Sow an action, reap a habit
Sow a habit, reap a character
Sow a character, reap a destiny

Ancient Chinese proverb

WEST:
Next we face the West, the place of Earth and matter. In the Southwest we 'dreamed', now, facing the West, we get to reap what we have dreamed. Thoughts are energy, and energy moves propelled by thought. Through deep introspection we shine the light of awareness on the world within, and thus get to see how we have manifested our outer world.

The authentic-self aspect of the West is acceptance of responsibility for one's life with no blame and no regret, no harking back, just full presence here and now. The egoic-self contains all those regrets, the blaming, and the little voice which says 'If only...........'

In the shadow of Little-Ego we become self absorbed, blinded by self-fixation, the ego trying to save itself from 'death'.

NORTHWEST:-
Next we face the Northwest power which relates to the making of rules and laws, justifications, 'shoulds, musts, oughts' and all that dogmatic stuff that can creep subtly into the mind. Are you limiting yourself by making rules for yourself based on past experience, or are you creatively daring to make new rules that support you in your life today? The negative rules are those we make for ourselves by which we govern, bind and limit our lives, our creativity, our rights, our sexual expression and so on, and keep habitual and familiar old pain-games and self-negating beliefs going.

From the authentic point of view the Northwest means acceptance of one's karma - action bringing re-action - as lessons we are here on earth to learn. Living without blame as a Warrior of the Spirit on a hero/ine's journey, walking with courage, bringing beauty with you wherever you go.

NORTH:
Facing the North we look at our mental belief systems and philosophies, what we think with the 'calculator' brain. The egoic side of the North is ungrounded theories and mental abstractions, bullshit ideas not grounded in knowing but motivated by beliefs taken on from others without actual experience.

The authentic aspect is that elusive quality of instinctual 'knowing', of being in alignment with spirit, in balance with the forces of the cosmos, in harmony with the way things are intended to be, in the present moment and not out there trying to make things fit a plan from ego. Culture and language are a web of agreed-upon notions developed over generations by tacit agreement through which we perceive and which we learn to use to communicate with and relate to others. Wisdom is knowing that's all they are, bullshit is believing that's how it really, categorically and absolutely is!

NORTHEAST:
The place of choice, of design and choreography of energy. How we choose and thereby design and choreograph our lives is the meat of the Northeast. The egoic aspect is unconscious choices or choices made with a sub-agenda of self-sabotage, those repetitive un-(or semi-)conscious choices that re-create old pain situations and traumas according to our psycho-cultural conditioning. Sometimes one can watch another person making horrendous choices that you just know will work out all wrong, and you also know it is no good saying anything because you will just be rejected or bring down a hail of abuse upon your head. Sometimes we humans just have to learn from our mistakes - and keep making them until the results are tough enough for us learn from.

The Light of the Northeast relates to the highest potential within ourselves. When we make our choices from the highest place within, we live with relaxed ease, with synchronicity, with maximum effect for good and minimum effort expended in relation to what is achieved. In this way we re-invent ourselves in every moment and are no longer creatures of automatic habit and stimulus-response.

EAST: -
The East is where all that has taken place so far around the wheel brings us to the payoff. The sower reaps either illumination ('Aha!') or else confusion, delusion and grief. ('Oh shit!')

Let us go quickly around the wheel in reverse and see more of how this works.

In the Circle Of The Authentic-Self the East means the reaping of illumination, 'seeing', Aha - got it! This comes from healthy life-affirmative and courageous choices (NE), following a sense of inner knowing (N), through trancendence of limiting rules for self and life (NW), acceptance of responsibility for my situation (W), through dreaming a positive dream of my real deep desires for the life I desire to live (SW), which I can do after accepting myself as a person of worth and value who dares to live in a relationship of trust and innocence with the Universe. (S).

In the circle of the egoic-self, it means that I reap grief and lack of self-worth (E) –through limited self-sabotaging choices (NE), mental confusion and refusal to face what I don't want to face (N), restrictive rules and laws put upon myself (NW), blaming of others to avoid my own responsibility (W), muddled and self-sabotaging dreaming (SW) and 'poor me' stuck-in-child mythologies (S). The payoff is that I don't have to take responsibility for my life, face my truth or deal with the consequences of what I have created.

SOUTHEAST:
The Southeast direction relates to our self concepts - how we feel about ourselves when the chips are down. When we create our life pandering to our shadow, protecting Little-Ego from seeing his true self, we have little self-worth and feel bad inside.

When we take courage and create our life according to our deepest inner desires and wishes, When we value and esteem ourselves and therefore value and esteem others and life itself, then we feel good, worthy and an honourable part of Creation. We ally our individual self with the Greater-Self and become no longer separate and alone, but connected with All-That-Is. Alone becomes All-One.

THE CIRCLE OF THE EGOIC SELF
CIRCLE OF FOXES
Now Let us look in more detail at the Star Maiden's Circle starting with its 'shadow' egoic manifestation known as 'THE CIRCLE OF FOXES'.

See if this circle reflects how you have been at any time in your life.

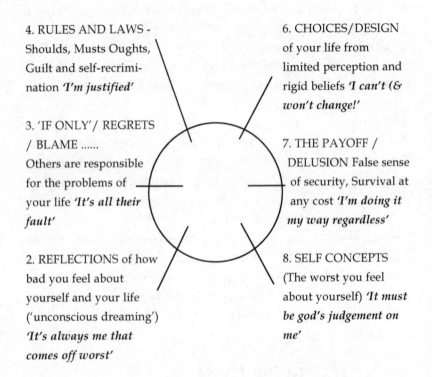

5. NEGATIVE BELIEFS ABOUT YOURSELF
Restricted selective perceptions
'I'M RIGHT!'

4. RULES AND LAWS -
Shoulds, Musts Oughts,
Guilt and self-recrimi-
nation *'I'm justified'*

3. 'IF ONLY'/ REGRETS / BLAME ......
Others are responsible
for the problems of
your life *'It's all their fault'*

2. REFLECTIONS of how
bad you feel about
yourself and your life
('unconscious dreaming')
'It's always me that comes off worst'

6. CHOICES/DESIGN
of your life from
limited perception and
rigid beliefs *'I can't (& won't change!'*

7. THE PAYOFF / DELUSION False sense
of security, Survival at
any cost *'I'm doing it my way regardless'*

8. SELF CONCEPTS
(The worst you feel
about yourself) *'It must be god's judgement on me'*

1. NEGATIVE 'MYTHOLOGIES' OF YOURSELF
Destructive inner dialogue. The negative stories you tell yourself.
'Poor me, I'm the victim'

WE BEGIN THE CIRCLE OF FOXES BY FACING SOUTH.

South - Mythology of self
"Poor me, I'm not good enough, I fear I never match up, I don't deserve, I'm the victim, they all do it to me. I feel guilty if I receive anything worth while. Anyone stupid enough to think I'm OK must be an idiot...."
We can fall into the trap of 'entertaining' ourselves with repet-

itive confirmations of our failures and inadequacies and the seeming difficulties and impossibilities of life.

(When asked 'how are you', there is a peculiarly British way of saying 'Fine, thank you', full of defensiveness. What 'fine' then means is "F = Fucked up, I = insecure, N = neurotic, and E = emotionally disturbed!")

Southwest - The 'dream'
Life manifests according to how we 'dream' it and then 'proves' us right:- *'This is true because look what happens to me constantly out in the world. People are always getting at me, putting me down, showing me I am not good enough, making me feel I'm undeserving. It just proves it all the time. I don't know why I bother. (And in extremis - 'I'll kill myself - that'll really show 'em. Then they will be sorry'.)* Prophecies become self-fulfilling. Rage that is unexpressed ends up as damage against the self.

West - The 'daydream' - the way it actually works out. The place of regrets and blame.
'If only... my childhood had been different, if my parents had loved me. It's all their fault really, I can't help being the way I am. If only people treated me decently now I wouldn't feel so undeserving. But I'm not going to give them another chance, I'll just hide myself away quietly!' (Or alternatively: *- If there's any messing, I'll get them before they get me.)*

All children are wounded, it is a natural and unavoidable part of life. No parent is perfect, it is sufficient to be a 'good enough' parent. Growing up means shifting from a victim perspective to taking responsibility for oneself.

Northwest - Rules and Laws
'My rules are that people are out to reject me, that I am undeserving, that if I show who I am I will be rejected - and I am so it must be true.'

Guilt and shame live here along with 'should, must and ought'.

North - Beliefs and philosophies
"I'm justified being the way I am. They're all against me anyway. I

believe I am right and I am, it is proved over and over again. Nothing is going to change, the world has no proper place for me and that's that".

When we are stuck in self-pity, we lose our sense of humour and tend to get righteous, prissy and defensive. In its extreme, this is the cradle of fascism and fanaticism - compleat believers who 'must' impose their beliefs on everyone else - for everyone else's own good, of course! The insecure find a false sense of security amongst hordes of other fellow fundamentalist believers.

Northeast - Choice, design and choreography of life

"I make my choices in life according to my beliefs and my rules. OK, it may not be a very rewarding life, but it's the one I've got. I organise my life so as to avoid pain, so as to survive somehow, and I do."

To stay comfortably asleep, we need to blame others, the world, politicians and/or God, for forcing choices on us, or making the choices that we really want to make seem impossible.

East - the grand delusion - the payoff

"What's in it for me? I do it my way. I survive. I avoid pain as much as posssible. I don't get love but that's not coming to me anyway. My parents didn't want me and no one else does either. I am a mistake and what d'you mean that's self-pity? Well, wouldn't you feel this way if you had suffered the way I have?" The payoff is avoidance of pain and a false sense of security.

Southeast - Self-concepts.

"Feel about myself? Don't ask."

How you feel about yourself inside when there is nothing and no one to prop you up, no one to impress, when you are alone in the middle of the night with nothing between you and the nitty-gritty of reality, shows you how much your old myths will benefit from work, from examination, and from reframing.

THE CIRCLE OF THE AUTHENTIC SELF.
'Dance of Coyotes'

ALIGNMENT WITH INNER KNOWING
Harmony and balance in the mind
'I seek knowledge and wisdom'

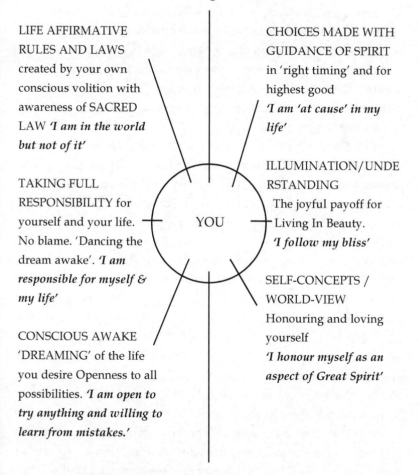

LIFE AFFIRMATIVE RULES AND LAWS created by your own conscious volition with awareness of SACRED LAW *'I am in the world but not of it'*

CHOICES MADE WITH GUIDANCE OF SPIRIT in 'right timing' and for highest good *'I am 'at cause' in my life'*

TAKING FULL RESPONSIBILITY for yourself and your life. No blame. 'Dancing the dream awake'. *'I am responsible for myself & my life'*

ILLUMINATION/UNDERSTANDING The joyful payoff for Living In Beauty. *'I follow my bliss'*

YOU

SELF-CONCEPTS / WORLD-VIEW Honouring and loving yourself *'I honour myself as an aspect of Great Spirit'*

CONSCIOUS AWAKE 'DREAMING' of the life you desire Openness to all possibilities. *'I am open to try anything and willing to learn from mistakes.'*

RE-INVENTING / RE-MYTHOLOGISING YOURSELF
Becoming / being the person you choose to be.
'I can become who and what I want'

Coyote is the trickster who sets traps and then falls into them, who looks at things upside down or backwards and generally screws up. Coyote is the Mulla Nasrudin of the Americas. In the Native American mythology, Coyote is the only approximation to the 'devil' of Christian teaching. Lucifer the Light Bringer is closer to the image of Coyote, but the 'devil' is, from the shamanic point of view, a perverted image. This is a major difference in how Christians and Shamanists see the world.

If you have separated 'God' into all good and no evil, you have to have a 'devil' to explain the bad things that happen. For the older cultures, creation was never split in this way and the 'Dark' and the 'Light' are seen in perfect partnership to make the whole. But things go 'wrong', we are imperfect, we make mistakes, bad things happen in all kingdoms, Mother Earth herself erupts in volcanoes, tornadoes blow, calamities happen. We humans make careful plans and all sorts of things go awry. 'Coyote' gets in and screws it all up! This is part of the plan of Creation. Coyote is the teacher who brings us to face ourself, to grow ourself, and who brings us to the path of spiritual development.

If everything went right, how would we have any challenge? Imagine a day going completely right from the moment you get out of bed. (OK, OK, maybe that sounds pretty good!) But imagine the next day, and the next, and the next, and everything goes absolutely perfectly and effortlessly, and soon you know that everyday for the rest of your life everything is going to be perfect and easy and effortless.......... wouldn't you just mess something up after a bit just for fun? Or just to know you are still living? Or to obviate the boredom of certainty? The storyline of the movie 'Groundhog day' made this point humourously.

We are each of us heroes and heroines on our journey of life. However, without challenge, without 'baddies', how can we be heroic and good? How can we learn the difference? Without the balance, life on Mother Earth makes no sense. I mean - would you buy a Harry Potter book if Lord Voldemort and all the Slytherins were not around and Harry just had a nice easy year at Hogwarts with nothing much happening?? Life on earth teaches us about right and wrong, about heroism and cowardice, about the consequences of our actions, and it constantly challenges us to learn and grow and to consciously take responsibility for ourselves and our lives.

APPLYING THESE QUALITIES TO THE WHEEL....

South: Instead of negative mythologies and beliefs, we choose to be who and what we really want to be by application of will, intent and focus. We consciously re-mythologise our-self and let go of the old familiar self-negating stories, pain-games, habits, addictions, cultural conditionings and so on. We re-invent ourself in the Light of Awareness and reclaim our Authentic Self. We are then ready to learn through pleasure in living and giving, and we are available to experience what life, the Great Mystery, serves up for us. We become the hero/ine of our own life journey.

Facing Southwest, we take the stand of being open to all possibilities and experiences rather than governed by how it used to be or what 'they' will approve or disapprove of. We set out to consciously 'dream' into manifestation the life of our choice, always understanding that in this realm there is a time lag for a 'dream' to become 'real' in the three dimensional world and there are other 'dreams' going on too that may interact with, or interfere with, our own. We set practical goals and work consistently to manifest them.

In the West, we choose to take responsibility for ourself, to stop daydreaming life away, and blaming others for our own situation. 'If only's' are exchanged for creative action. The West is the place of earth and the physical and so we get grounded instead of living in fantasy. The child-shield is healed by 'passing through the body of the Great Mother'. We learn to take responsibility and begin to actualize our dreams and become co-creators of our own destiny.

In the Northwest, we touch on Sacred Law, the Laws of the Universe, of God, instead of getting bogged down with the societal mores of the day. We consciously make the choice to separate ourself from other people's 'shoulds, musts and oughts', and guilt that is provoked as a means to control us. This is not easy and extracts a price, as all personal psycho-spiritual growth and development does. The price is that one is no longer part of the society in quite the same way. Others may not sense much change right away, but you may feel a sense of loneliness/aloneness inside. Beware, though, if your ego gets off on the idea of being different and special and wants to tell people about it - that just means you are more the same than ever!

In the North we seek to touch our innate sense of knowing and to maintain openness to all knowledge and a questioning of all beliefs. We stop pre-judging people and situations and we are ready to dare to go with the flow of the seeming co-incidences of life and the nudges of Spirit. We maintain a state of 'beginners mind'. How we make sense of life will change with the shift of inner mythology, and we may find that we start to experience things from new points of view. In this direction, the child-shield is healing by 'passing through the body of the father'.

Facing Northeast we can then make new choices from a place of inner balance and harmony. These can be free choices to act in the world instead of react, to choose from a self-myth of a balanced, co-operative, harmonious self, instead of the old self-pitying, combative, victimised 'poor-me'.

In the East direction there is no longer any payoff or hidden agendas as nothing is hidden and we can open our imagination, the 'realm of the magician', to unlimited possibilities. This means opening to our spiritual vision to the Light, following our bliss, re-creating our life anew with acceptance of full responsibility for it.

In the Southeast we find that our self-concepts have made a mega-transformation and our attitudes and approach to life become fundamentally renewed and gloriously life-affirmative and joyful.

That is the plan! That is the map of the journey. But while a good map is a great help and gets us started, the JOURNEY STILL HAS TO BE UNDERTAKEN A STEP AT A TIME.

So forgive yourself for not being enlightened all at once and set out to WALK THE BEAUTY WAY With Dedication, Perseverance and a Spirit of Joy!

THE WALK OF THE WOLF

BRIDGES ACROSS THE CIRCLE

The Walk of the Wolf is another interesting way of approaching the Star Maiden's Circle.

It is about working with the pairs of opposites. As you read this you may like to place yourself in the directions and walk across the diagonals of the wheel, feeling the powers and your relationship to them.

Note: The following is to some extent a repetition of information given previously in Section One part 3. However there is so much to impart that I feel it is worth taking another look from a different point of view and adding further knowledge.

SOUTH-NORTH BRIDGE - THE RED ROAD: The South is the place of our wounded child, the needy, victim part of ourselves that may be locked in past mythologies of pain and fear, and usually needs the most healing. We begin to heal by facing those fears and daring to walk in trust and innocence, letting natural curiosity take us out into the world, daring to be emotionally open and vulnerable, crying if we are sad, expressing anger when angry instead of hiding it away till it becomes resentment, laughing and letting our natural joy manifest, being in the here and now with just what is.

Then we can make a bridge to the North, the everyday adult part of us that looks after the future, that when grown up is guided by true wisdom and inner knowing rather than theories and the mistaken 'clarity' of the know-all. In so many of us, it has been our adult-self who, with internalised parental and other voices from past times, beats the hell out of the inner child, reinforcing the old woundings. When we can harmonize these two aspects of ourselves in beauty, we are on the way to learning to walk in balance guided by the heart. This is the essential teaching of the RED ROAD.

SOUTHWEST-NORTHEAST BRIDGE - THE 'YELLOW ROAD': The Southwest is the place of our 'dreams', our desires for our life that we seek to manifest into external reality. Many of us do not allow ourselves to 'dream' and sabotage ourselves through hidden self-negating beliefs. The work of this direction is to clarify our purpose and focus our intent on what we really want. Then we can cross to the Northeast place of choice and design and make the decisions that will move us towards actualizing our desires. In this way we can 'dance our dreams awake' in beauty, and give our gifts to the world. Nothing brings a human being greater happiness than giving our gifts freely and having them received and acknowledged.

THE WEST-EAST BRIDGE - THE BLUE ROAD: This bridge unites dark and light, matter and spirit, incarnation and imagination. Here spirit becomes substance and substance moves back to spirit. All that we can imagine, we can potentially make into 'reality'. All human dreams begin with imagination, vision, conception (East) which can then be birthed into material reality (West). Through incarnate experience, we human spirits get the opportunity to act out our imaginations in material reality and get constant feedback on how we are doing and the effects of what we create. In the egoic circle, ungrounded fantasy (west) led us to a state of delusion - with a hidden payoff we didn't want to admit to ourself (East). Now, acting through our authentic self, we take full responsibility for our life experience in the realm of matter-reality without a hidden agenda or negative payoff. We can now be open to the incredible range of our illumined imagination and our creative possibilities. This is the essence of the *BLUE ROAD*.

The last bridge is NORTHWEST TO SOUTHEAST – THE 'BROWN ROAD'. The Northwest is the place of patterns, habits, rules, laws, and the feedback action of karma. (Karma simply means that all action brings reaction.) Opposite is the southeast place of self-concepts, which we learn from our history (i.e. Everything before the moment of now.) and our ancestry / family of origin.

Our self-concepts will echo the rules and laws we make for our-self and vice-versa. If we feel guilt, it will affect how we feel about our-self. The more we can release learned baggage of guilt, shame and blame and align our personal rules and laws with Sacred Law (i.e. The way it really is) rather than human prejudice and cultural mores, the easier we will be on ourself and the more affirmative our self-concepts will become. We move towards becoming a Warrior of the Spirit, able to *Walk Our Talk* in balance and harmony with all directions.

Please note: The RED ROAD & BLUE ROAD are original Native American names. The appellations - Yellow Road and Brown Road come from my friend and co-worker Dawn Russell.

SUMMARY OF THE POWERS TO YOUR LEFT, TO YOUR RIGHT, AND OPPOSITE
Around the Circle to expand understanding

Starting in the SOUTHEAST. Here you sit in the place of your history, which is all that has gone before the moment of now, and your ancestors whose line has given birth to you and whose gifts and burdens you carry in your body and blood. To your right is your spirit (and your spirit-history) that existed before you took on this physical life and that will continue to exist after it is finished. To your left is the child within, the part of you that is most effected by your human inheritance as it is you before you began development and work on yourself. Opposite you are the patterns and karma that reflect both your spiritual and physical inheritances.

Sitting in the SOUTH. On your right hand in the Southeast are your ancestors and your history, all that has formed you and your patterns. On your left in the Southwest is your 'dream' and the reflections that daily life gives you. How you sit in your South is influenced by your inheritance and your past and is expressed in how you manifest your dream, which is reflected back to you by daily life. So simple once you understand it!

Opposite you is your North place of the adult and how you think and express yourself in today's world.

Now move to the SOUTHWEST. Sitting here in your place of the dream, your right hand is in your South, your inner child, and your left in your West, the physical domain where you experience manifest reality. Your ability to dream (Southwest),and to manifest what you want, is a measure of how you have healed your personal history, the wounds of your inner child, and how much you have developed the gifts and blessings you inherited. This is constantly reflected to you by what you manifest.

Opposite, in the Northeast, is your place of choice and design of life. Your decisions reflect your dream, and your dreaming affects your decisions.

Next the WEST. Now you sit in the place of the physical and of what is manifested, the place of your body, the earth's body, the body of all that you experience as solid reality. Your experience in this place is a direct expression of your 'dream'. This means both what you have consciously dreamed and what you have unconsciously dreamed. If you don't like your life, dream a new dream!

Shamans from the old cultures say we, the 'younger brother' are dreaming the wrong dream and it is going to collapse around our ears, it is an unsustainable dream, out of kilter and destructive to our Mother, the Earth. This is quite obvious to all thinking, feeling, listening, truly sentient people. To dream a new dream we have to go back and start in the South to heal the wounds that cause the faulty dreaming, and then dream a whole lot more consciously and carefully. The West is where you get life's feedback, daily experience in the mirror of external reality.

Your left hand is in the Northwest place of pattern and karma - the patterns you have inherited which run your life according to the degree that you have mastered them or they still master you - and the karmic lessons you elected to face on this earth journey. This also feeds into your manifest experience of the everyday. In the West you get full-monty feedback and reflection!

Opposite you is the East place of spirit. How much you let spirit in, or shut the whole idea out, deeply affects your experience of everyday reality, through how much you are connected to the deeper subtle realities – the hidden matrix of interconnected life –

or how much you feel alone and isolated, surviving amongst imagined or real enemies.

Now to the NORTHWEST. Sitting here your right hand is in manifest reality of the West and your left hand is in the thinking adult place of the North. You sit in the place of patterns – opposite you is the Southeast place of the ancestors and history from whence your patterns come. (Remember 'history' means everything up to this moment.)

How you work with your inherited patterns is reflected to you from your right by the West and feeds into your daily adult life at your left through your knowledge and wisdom and also your inherited beliefs and unthinking acceptance of views of others. From this comes the rules and laws you make, mainly un- or semi-consciously, for the daily running of your life, the limitations and controls you put on what you may do and who, of your many possible selves, you may allow yourself to be.

Sitting in the NORTH, you sit in your place of adulthood and of the battle between real knowledge, wisdom, balance and harmony and their surrogate imposters such as beliefs taken on from the mainstream without intelligent critical discernment. To you right are the patterns which influence how you think, and to your left is the place of choice, which is how you express your thoughts though actions. Opposite you is your South, your inner child with its gifts and its wounds. How emotionally mature you are, how much you have worked to master your inherited patterns, and how much wisdom you have attained directly affect the choices you make and the life you thereby create for yourself.

Moving to the NORTHEAST, you sit in your place of choice and design of life energy. Opposite you is your dream of life, your thoughts, desires, prayers and intentions. To your right is your adult thinking and conceptualizing self and to your left is your spirit and higher self. How you choose is all important in the creation of your life and how you do or do not manifest your dreams depends on the choices you make.

There is a common saying – 'make up your mind'. But if we do that it means we focus our choice on the information at our right hand only, the information supplied by our thinking self. And we put our mind in the place of dominance rather than as our servant. We become super-rational-person. Much better to use our mind for its proper purpose - to sort and sift information, to prepare and draft the possibilities and the likely effects of such actions – and then to call spirit from our left hand and use all our intuition and subtle knowing to guide our plan of action and help us make our choices.

So – the recommendation from the world of the medicine wheel is –

NEVER MAKE UP YOUR MIND AGAIN,
USE YOUR MIND TO SIFT AND SORT BUT CONSULT SPIRIT
FOR YOUR DECISIONS

Lastly, move to the EAST. Here you sit in the place of spirit, fire, of the high view of Eagle, of passion for life, of the 'fire within'. To your right is choice and design of life and to your left is your ancestors and your history. This is the beginning and ending place as it is where you come from – from spirit – and from where, as spirit, you enter the matrix of life through taking on a body with an ancestral line – your left hand – and it is also where you reap the rewards of your lived life. According to your choices, so you will advance from what you were given by your ancestors or you will fall into, and repeat, their same old traps. How connected you are to your spirit-essence (east) will be reflected to you in your everyday life experiences (west).

The circle is an interconnected whole and shows how all the powers act and interact on us and how we reap the work we do in our inner world in the everyday external world.

The Star Maiden's Circle maps our human process in a circular
form.

Once you have got the sense of it into you
so you know the meanings of each direction
without even having to think
which is not hard because it is
a completely natural sequence –
the wheel will 'live' inside you
and guide and help you in your daily life.

SECTION THREE

THE COSMOS REVEALED IN ALL ITS BEAUTY AND COMPLEXITY

The Earth Count

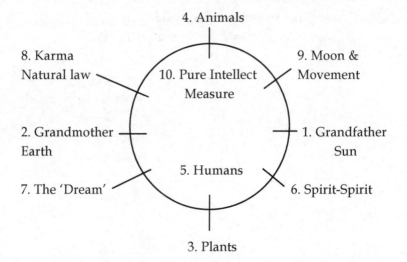

The Earth Count is an ancient way of teaching of the origins of the Universe that has been handed down to us by the Maya. It most probably pre-dates the Maya and comes via them from the ancient cultures of the time before the Great Flood. I have been taught this by Hyemeyohosts Storm, Harley Swiftdeer, Joan Halifax and other students of this path, in different ways, at different times and with different emphases. No one teaches it the same each time because it is not a dogma, but a Living Myth. Today I will say it like this.............

In the beginning was the Great Round, the Zero, the No-Thing which is the potential of All Things, the Womb of all Life that births All Existence. All the Children of Creation are designed in the Zero and from the Zero come forth into manifestation.

The Zero is the Marriage of All-That-Is-Feminine -Great

Grandmother Wakan - and   All-That-Is-Masculine - Great Grandfather Ssquan, the Lightningbolt who potentises the zero of potential into manifestation.

Now, in the little part of the Universe which we humans inhabit......

Great Grandmother Wakan and Great Grandfather Ssquan made love and gave birth to their first born, Grandfather Sun.

Grandfather Sun is given the number One. From our point of view He rises in the East, so we place him on the Medicine Wheel in the Easterly Direction.

Great Grandfather and Great Grandmother made love a second time and gave birth to Grandmother Earth. Grandmother is given the number Two, and we place her opposite the Sun on the West of the Wheel.

Grandfather Sun and Grandmother Earth now made love and they gave birth to their first born, the Kingdom of Plants. The plants thrive in the summer and they depend on water so we place them in the South direction of the Wheel. Their number is Three which is the sum of One and Two.

Grandmother and Grandfather made love again and gave birth to their second born, the Kingdom of Animals. The animals breath the air and we place them on the North of the wheel. Their number is Four which is the sum of One and Two plus One.

Grandmother and Grandfather made love a third time and gave birth to their third born, the Kingdom of Humans. The place of the Humans is in the Centre of the Wheel but towards the South because Humans are as yet children of the Cosmos. We are the one kingdom that is still learning its potential. Our number is Five.

Number Six is called Spirit-Spirit because all things are born into substance from Spirit. In Spirit, there is no linear time, all time is One Gigantic Moment.

Six is the number of all directions: East, West, South, North, Above and Below. Six is Presence in life. This 'presence' in linear time comes from our history and our ancestry and it is from this that the life we experience in the 'present moment' is created. Our ancestors and our history are part of the power of six. Six is placed in the Southeast direction between fire and water.

Seven is the number of the six directions plus the power of Light (One). It is the 'Dream' of creation. In the energy of the Dream, there is no time and no matter, there is just the 'Dream of Life'. (Quantum physicists have shown this, just as the shamans have said for millennia and Shakespeare four hundred years ago!) The 'Dream' is placed on the Wheel in the Southwest, between Earth and Water, and its number is Seven.

Eight is the number of pattern and repetition, cycles and circles, physical laws. It is the 'form' of the 'dream'. Eight is the number for the Natural Law of the Universe, for Karma - the power of action-brings-reaction - which maintains balance and harmony in all things. Eight is placed in the Northwest between earth and air.

Nine is the number for Movement and Change. It is the number for Sister Moon who moves the tides and winds of Earth, and moves the tidal waves of blood within all living beings who have hearts and the power of movement. Nine is placed Northeast between air and fire.

Ten is the number for Pure Intellect and Measure of all material things. It is the power of Movement and Change (9) plus the Light (1). Ten is the number for our Spirit-Twin or Higher-Self. The ten is placed to the north of the centre of the wheel.

The Earth Count is the basis of the Twenty Count which now follows..........

THE TWENTY (CHILDREN'S) COUNT

The Twenty Count is the foundation Medicine Wheel and it stands behind all the teachings I have written of so far. The Twenty Count is a Circle of Mirrors and a story of Creation. It follows directly from the first creation story in the prologue and from the Earth Count and begins with the same numbers as the Earth Count and expands our understanding of these powers.

THE CARDINAL 'HOLDER' POINTS OF THE WHEEL.

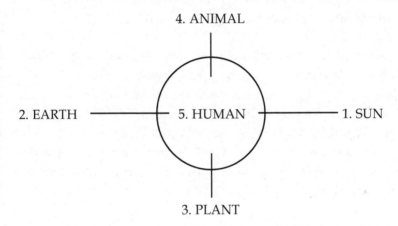

4. ANIMAL

2. EARTH — 5. HUMAN — 1. SUN

3. PLANT

1. Sun. Fire. Genitals.

Great Grandmother WAKAN and Great Grandfather SSQUAN made love and gave birth to their firstborn, Grandfather SUN, our Great Father. His is the power of light, illumination, fire and warmth, the power that 'sees far' and lights up all things. He is the part of the primal Fire Of Creation around which, and as part of which, we have our life and our being.

The power of One is the power of Eagle who 'sees far', the power of vision, of enlightenment, of fire and lightning, it is our illumination, our imagination – our 'I-Mage' – the magician within, our connection to the World of Spirit, to All-That-Is-Above, to the Galaxy and the Universe.

One is also our genitals, the egg of the woman and the semen of the man, and the wondrous magic power of sexual fire and love through which we are all born.

2. Earth. Gaia, our planet. Minerals. Womb and testes. Will.

Great Grandmother and Great Grandfather made love a second time and their second born is Grandmother Earth, our True Mother and source of our physical being. She holds the power of intro-spection, of 'Looks Within'. Out of her has come our bodies, our temples, within which Spirit can dwell in third dimensional reality, our 'vehicles of experience' through which we perceive this level of vibration so that we experience it as solid and real. We are walking earth, our bones are as stone, our flesh is as soil, and our blood is as water.

The power of two holds the powers of intuition, of death and darkness, of transformation, of deep knowledge from within, the Underworld, the power that underlies manifest existence, of all that 'matters'. This is our place of connection to All-That-Is-Below, to the World Of Ancestral Spirits and Spirit Beings of the Earth.

Two is the woman's womb and the man's testes and it is the power of the will. The greatest power of will is to create life and together, female and male, we can do that.

3. Kingdom of the plants. Water. Stomach. Emotions.

Now Grandmother and Grandfather made love and gave birth to their firstborn, the Kingdom of the Plants. The plants are stationary consciousness and they constantly seek to grow and to give of themselves without reservation. They have the power to change death into life. They die to give of themselves to feed us, cloth us, build our dwellings, give fire for our warmth, medicines for our health, and special hallowed medicines to assist us with our under-standing of life.

In the South is the element of water and the blood that runs through our veins, and our emotional body through which we feel the world. The South power is trust and innocence, inner sense, our inner essense. In the human this inner place is - quite literally - the stomach. This is where the plants are transformed into energy, our life force. We feel our emotions in the stomach. What we eat affects our emotions, and our emotional state effects our ability to digest what we eat.

4. Kingdom of the animals. Air. Heart and lungs.
Grandfather and Grandmother made love a second time and gave birth to the Kingdom of the Animals. Their place is in the North of the wheel with the element of air and they have the gift of lungs, heart, brain and thought. Consciousness in the animals is no longer rooted and so movement is birthed. They are the ancestors of the humans. Many of them give their lives to feed and cloth us.

The North for us humans is the place of the instinctual knowledge of the heart, of balance and alignment, logic and harmony; also of thinking intelligence that is concerned with the future. It is also the centre of courage and fear, and we are challenged through life to face our fears and live with courage. How we do this determines how effectively all our other centres work.

5. Humans. Communication. Throat, mouth, tongue and taste.
Grandmother and Grandfather made love a third time and gave birth to their third born, the humans, ourselves, Our sacred number is five. We have the power of communication, language and of self-reflection, which sets us apart from other creatures. Our place on the wheel is in the Centre, but South of the Centre because we are as yet children, still learning to become fully human beings.

It is the gift of self-reflection, of knowing 'I', that marks the uniqueness of human consciousness. It brings with it the tremendous gift of self-knowledge, of knowledge of past and future, of knowledge of 'right' and 'wrong', and thus the enormous responsibility of conscious choice, with which comes the experience and knowledge of karma – that all action brings re-action. We have the ability to conceptualise, to create and commu-nicate images and symbols. We can communicate everything from the deepest wisdom to the most banal stupidity!

To one, the Sun, the Fire of Creation, add four, the animal, to create five, the self-reflective consciousness of the human. Or to put it another way, an animal reaches into the fire, the light of creation - illumination - and gains the consciousness of self-reflection and so becomes a human.

Hu means divine and man means mortal. Hu-mans are divine mortals in that we have the gift of self knowledge, the knowledge that 'I Am'. The other kingdoms do not have that gift and so we are, in this specific sense, 'closer to the gods'.

However, the ancient teachings tell us that while plants are fully plants and animals are fully animals, we are yet to become fully human. We are on our Great Journey, learning through life experience to balance the forces of light and dark, to become 'Masters of Energy', to experience and know that we co-create our reality and that no-thing is actually here the way we perceive it. The teachings say that we are still children of the Cosmos and thus our place is in the South of the wheel until such time as we learn to work together, stop warring, grow up to spiritual adulthood and become Caretakers of the Earth and Each Other, living with knowledge and wisdom, in balance, alignment and harmony with our Planet and All-That-Is.

THE NON-CARDINAL 'MOVER' POINTS OF THE WHEEL.

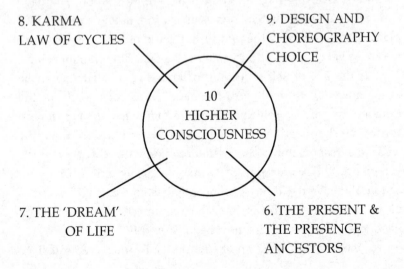

8. KARMA
LAW OF CYCLES

9. DESIGN AND
CHOREOGRAPHY
CHOICE

10
HIGHER
CONSCIOUSNESS

7. THE 'DREAM'
OF LIFE

6. THE PRESENT &
THE PRESENCE
ANCESTORS

6. The Present and the Presence. Ancestors. Eyes, ears and nose.
To the power of Five, the human being, add the light of One,
Grandfather Sun. All that is born into substance is born from Spirit.
In the timelessness of Spirit we are in the NOW, fully present.
Hence when we are fully conscious and present while in body here
on earth (not an easy achievement), we experience the Presence of
Life, our presence-in-life. Six is both ancestors and history, all that
has gone before that makes up our life in the present moment, and
it is the Present Moment itself. The Present is the sum total
produced by the past, it is the gift from the past. When a human
being is Fully Present in the Moment of Now, that human is awake
to the effect of all that is past.

All who have come before are our ancestors in whose paths we
follow. Through our ancestors we have come to exist. Our presence
is only possible because of the past, out of which we have been
created. Our ancestors live on through us - their blessings we
inherit and their problems become ours to heal.

The Six is also called Spirit-Spirit because all things are born
into substance from Spirit. In spirit, there is no linear time, all time
is One Gigantic Moment. Thus when a living human is Fully
Present in the Now, s/he is at one with the deeper reality of
timeless existence where all is now.

Six is the number of all directions: East, West, South, North,
Above and Below. It is through this centre that we experience both
visible and invisible worlds.

Hyemeyohsts Storm teaches that a human when centred in the
energy of five - the Centre of the Self - will live from his/her
Centre. When centred in 5 with the added power of one (illumination), a human becomes fully present as a centred human, a six.
However, if instead a human lives centred in sexuality and the
base center (1) - the human (5) will be subjugated by their sex and
security drives (1) and so will be present (6) in the world in a very
much lesser way.

7. The Dream of Life. Top of the head. Brain-mind.
We now add two - the Earth - to the power of Five - human

consciousness. When a human walks upon the earth, s/he is experiencing the 'Dream'. All physical life is vibration, waves or minute 'particles' that are not solid but are energy-in-motion. All matter is energy, all 'solid' matter is maya, illusion. We all know that earthlife seems very real and feels as if it is all solid and happening out there, but from the point of view of the shamanic way of understanding, 'no-thing' is really out there at all.

This is a very great paradox. The way of the shaman - and the way of all mystics under whatever title - is about 'seeing' through the illusion and experiencing the reality behind the apparent reality, 'seeing' beyond the description of reality, the consensual reality that we have been taught is the only one. The idea is to become able to experience the really real world as well as the apparently real one.

As Casteneda's don Juan says, we see only a description of the world and not the world itself. This is the 'Dream of Life' which, through the brain-mind, we experience as so real. Its place on the Wheel is Southwest, between earth and water, and its number is Seven.

The brain-mind - the physical organ of the brain - takes in information through the five senses and 'creates' the world we think we live in. This brain turns the waves of creation into an understandable and apparently-real world.

Seven is the number of the six directions plus the power of Light (1). It is the 'Dream Of Life'. It is also the human (5) experience of Life on Earth (2) in the illusion of linear time and apparently solid matter.

KARMA. LAWS OF CYCLES AND CIRCLES. SACRED AND NATURAL LAW. RELATIONSHIPS. Body-mind.

To the Five now add Three, the power of emotion - energy-motion, of trust and fear, of water and the plant kingdom. Through the experience of feeling the world, a human experiences karma, the law of cycles and circles, of action and reaction.

The eight is Laws of the Cosmos, Sacred Law, the laws of Creation, of balance and justice, and it is also man made laws and rules which are our efforts to create society. It is also the inner rules and laws we make for ourselves by which we conduct our lives, and which so frequently keep us in bondage to conditioned ways and ideas until such time as we dare to get them out of the closet and really look at them and redraft them to work creatively for us.

Karma is the word for action-brings-reaction, which is how we learn the lessons of life. The Universe serves lessons up to us over and over again to educate us. Once we learn the lesson, we turn our karma into dharma - walking in balance or 'Walking the Beauty Way'. Then a new lesson will come to us. And so it goes on and on.   And on!

Eight is the number of pattern and repetition, of morphogenetic fields. It is the form of the 'dream'. A human (5) experiences the flowing waters of emotion (3) and learns that action brings reaction. Eight is the number for Karma, the Natural Law of the Universe.   Plants (3) - of the garden - teach humans (5) of the Natural Laws of Earth.

In the morphogenetic field, all the cells have consciousness and participate in the creation and maintenance of the vehicle-of-experience we know as the body. This is the body-mind, the internal knowing. The brain-mind (7) is awake when we are awake and the body-mind is awake when we are asleep. Very occasionally both are awake at the same time and we experience magic moments of lucidity and power.

9. Design and choreography of energy. Moon and movement. Choice. The 'luminous egg' electromagnetic energy field of the body.

To the Five now add Four, the power of mind, of the wind and of the animal kingdom. A human being, through the reflective power of mind, experiences the power of conscious choice, the power to create and destroy, and experiences the effect of his/her actions through the feedback loop of karma.   We are the 'determiners' of energy and our job is to learn to use our power wisely, for the good of all.

Nine is the number for movement and change. It is the number for the Moon who moves the tides and winds of Earth and moves the tidal waves of blood within all living beings. A human (5) learns with intellect (4) to make choices and become a mover and designer of energy herself.

Right now, as supposed Caretakers of the Earth, we are on the verge of fouling our beloved nest. Right now our collective ability to use energy wisely is not great. We have much to learn and we seem only to be able to learn from our mistakes. It seems that only by putting ourselves right up against the threat of self-extinction are we perhaps going to be able to make the creative choices necessary to live in balance and harmony with each other, with the other kingdoms and with the Planet Herself, in caring co-operation rather than heartless competition.

10. Higher consciousness, expanded awareness, Higher Self, spirit-knowing, pure intellect, measure of all intellect.

To Five we now add another Five. The Ten is known as 'Measure of all intellect'.Intellect is the ability to measure in the widest sense and together with this ability comes higher consciousness, expanded awareness, 'spirit-knowing'. The ten is the power of collective consciousness, of the 'Higher-Self/higher-consciousness' that can know the bigger picture and is connected to the source.

In Biblical terminology: "When two or three are gathered together in my name (which means nature - all Biblical names are descriptions of the nature of the person or place) there shall I be also." When two or more of us are gathered together with spiritual intent to access higher consciousness, there shall Higher-Consciousness (Spirit) be also.

We humans are self-reflective beings on our journey to becoming whole, the fully realised consciousness, one with the Father-Mother Force-of-Creation. We are the centre of the wheel of fire, earth, air and water. For us, these four directions are our spirit, our body, our mind and our emotions. It is good for us humans to remember that the other kingdoms all came before us, have lived longer than us, and without them we would not have life. Without the humble garden worm the soil would not be aerated and ready for plants to find what they need to grow, and we humans would starve.

Ten is the number for Pure Intellect and Measure of all material things. It is the Human (5) plus other human (5), the mirror reflection of self. It is the power of movement and change (9) plus the light (1) of awareness. Ten is the number for our Spirit-twin from whom we separated at birth and with whom we reunite at death.

NOW WE ADD THE POWER OF TEN -
AND MOVE UP AN OCTAVE

THE HIGHER OCTAVE: 11 TO 15

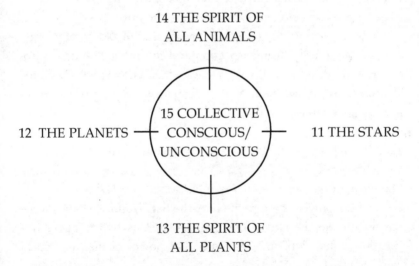

All the numbers of the wheel add up, subtract, multiply and divide, and through this, they teach knowledge of relationship.

11. THE STARS. ALL THE SUNS. Sister Moon. Time, memory, inspiration.
One is our own Sun, so Eleven is All-The-Suns, the stars. It is the

spirit essence of all suns, of fire, light and illumination.

The Eleven is also time, and memory that begins with time. Time begins when suns are born. Before that, time is not. And it is our Moon who rules our cycles and changes. Hence, for us, the eleven means higher illumined knowledge. (Or it's shadow partner - delusion). Eleven is one - illumination, plus ten - higher consciousness. Illumined knowledge through higher states of consciousness. Inspiration.

Eleven is 8 - patterns of life, plus 3 - life itself, the plant kingdom (Life as we know it begins with the plants) = Patterns of all lifetimes (Stored in memory.)

Moon, (11), by her movements, creates the cyclic patterns (8) of plants (3) through which they grow, flower and die.

3 - the quality of Trust and Innocence and seeking of perfection, plus 8 - Karma, the teachings in the Book of Life that we have come to earth to experience, give life-time and memory.

To 9 - our ability to choose and the quality of design of energy, add 2 - the quality of introspection and intuition. Through introspection we design our life with enlightened knowledge. Or on the shadow side, if we choose our life path without proper introspection, we land up in delusion.

12. All the planets. Organisation. Intuitive spirit-consciousness

Planets are organisers of energy into form.

Add the power of ten to the two, the Earth, and we have all the Earths, all the life supporting planets. Just as two is our introspection / intuition, so 12 is the higher power of that, our spirit consciousness.

Adding 10 - higher consciousness - to 2 – 'looking within', means conscious living. It means walking in balance on the earth, letting go of fantasy, being in the here and now, living in a way that is spiritually connected to the underlying patterns unfolding in the Universe.

12 is written with 1 and 2 which = 3, our feelings which open us to trust and innocence and to intuition, illumination and spirit

consciousness.

12 is 9 - choreography and design of life-energy, plus 3 - all plants, i.e. life. The choreography of life itself according to spirit consciousness of Mother Earth.

12 is 8 - cycles of life in the circle of law, plus 4 - all animals, who live in balance with those cycles. We humans have not yet learned to live in balance with natural law. When we have straightened our mental abilities and learned to walk in wisdom (the Light side of our 4), then we too will be in balance with our 12 and no longer threatening the destruction of the eco-system of the earth.

12 is 7 - the dream, plus 5 - humans. It is the 'dreamspace' created by Planet Earth for humans to live and learn in.

Twelve is 1, the Sun, plus 11, time and memory. Shining the light of illumination upon our memory and the knowledge gained through times past can bring us spirit-consciousness.

13. Spirit of all plants. White Buffalo Woman. Transformation.
Life - death – rebirth - Cycles of movement. Constancy of change -

Adding the spirit (10) of all plants (3) - the green of the earth - makes 13, the Spirit Of All Plants. Every plant is a cell in the body of 13.

This can be likened to the 'Virgin Mary'. Virgin means woman/feminine in her full potential (Nothing whatever to do with sex - that is one of the alterations to our mythology that has made life unnecessarily difficult in this culture). Look for a moment at the word MARY. Mary - mare - mater - matter - mother. The Virgin Mary is mare, the ocean through which all life begins (no water, no life), she is Mater, the mother, the material, she is Earthmother, the giver of all life. For the Native Americans, 13 is White Buffalo Woman / Goddess Beauty / Goddess Nature / Death Mother.

All plants, every grass, tree, flower, herb, vegetable, seaweed, growing thing, is a cell in the great body of the Virgin Mary / White Buffalo Woman / Earthmother, and each has its cycle of living and dying and living again.

13 is 9 - our choice and design of energy, plus 4 - our wisdom (or otherwise). We create our 'dream-life' through our mind, the power of our thought, our imagination, and the choices we make.

13 is 3 - a plant food, say an apple, plus 10 - the spirit-consciousness of that apple. Eat the apple and the apple itself dies and the spirit-consciousness is released. We feed on the spirit of the plant. Hence it is good to eat real, 'live' food. Junk food is dead, it has matter but no spirit. We may feel fed and full but we are actually starving.

For humans, just as 3 is the wounded child struggling in fear, so 13 is the place of waking up and transforming the wound into the wellspring of renewal. Adding 10, higher consciousness to 3, the child, means 'dying' to the old self, 'erasing personal history'. Letting go of all those old patterns of the past, of self negation, self-pity, old addictions, fantasies, self defeating choices etc, and transforming the inner patterns that brought them into being into patterns of beauty and joy.

13 is 10 + 3 and 13 is 1+3 = 4. The Earthmother gives her spiritual food, the spirit (10) of all plants(3), to feed all 4's, the animals, including the animal part of us humans.

13 is 7 + 6. For us humans, 7 - the 'dream' happening now, plus 6 - our history, all that has gone before now, makes 13 - our everchanging 'dream' – the life-death-rebirth-cycles of existence.

Or 13 is 5 - our humanness, plus 8 - cycles of life / karma. Together this makes our personal 'dream', our individual life-death-rebirth cycle.

14 . Spirit Of All Animals, Sweet Medicine. Natural knowing. Our alignment with All-That-Is

Add the spirit (10) to animals (4) and we have the Spirit Of All Animals (14). This is Sky Father, White Buffalo, the masculine God-figure. Every animal, all four leggeds, flyers, crawlers, swimmers are cells in the great body of fourteen, known as 'Sweet Medicine'.

As 13 is the Great Feminine Archetype, so 14 is the Great Masculine Archetype. In the Western world of today these powers are greatly out of balance.

For humans, the 14 is our resonance and alignment with All-That-Is. Our in (or out-of) tuneness with Great Spirit. Our instinctual intellect.

14 is 1 + 4 = 5, our self-reflective human consciousness that gives us the potential to embody harmonic resonance and alignment with All Creation.

14 is 9 - the power of choice and design, plus 5 - a human being. According to our humanness (5) and our ability to choose well (9), we manifest our degree of alignment and harmony (or otherwise) with The-Everything.

14 is 8 - Circle Of Law, and 6 - our history. According to all that has gone before and how we are living our karma, so will be our degree of alignment and harmony with Life.

15. Souls of All Humans. Holographic Awareness. Collective Consciousness.

Add 10, Higher Consciousness, to the power of Five, the Human Being. 15 is Souls Of All Humans in and out of body, the totality of the human family. It is our collective conscious and unconscious minds, the total of the cosmic human thought-form. In this sense, All-That-Is is part of 'Me'. It is the great 'I-Am' of human self-reflective consciousness.

15 is 9 - choice and design of energy, plus 6 - our history, our ancestors. According to how our ancestors and ourselves have, up to now, designed life to be, so is the state of our human collective consciousness and experience of being.

15 is 7 - the dream, plus 8 - karma, our lessons on this earth. We, as an individual, contribute to the collective mind through our life experience and how we deal with our karma, our life lessons.

15 is 1 + 5 = 6. Presence/history. Souls experiencing the Presence of Life. All that has gone before brings us to our collective consciousness now.

15 is 12 plus 3. Intuitive Spirit-Consciousness plus Trust & Innocence and our seeking of perfection (or fear and imperfection) of all of us adds up to our total collective consciousness the way it is.

THE HIGHER OCTAVE: 16 TO 20

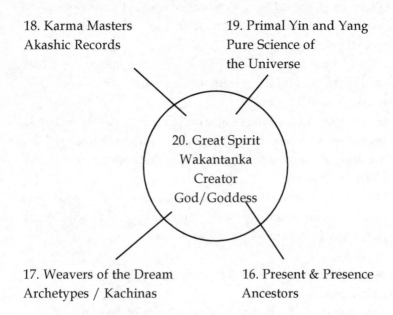

18. Karma Masters
Akashic Records

19. Primal Yin and Yang
Pure Science of
the Universe

20. Great Spirit
Wakantanka
Creator
God/Goddess

17. Weavers of the Dream
Archetypes / Kachinas

16. Present & Presence
Ancestors

16. GREAT PRESENCES. ENLIGHTENED ANCESTORS, AVATARS.

Synchonicity. Co-incidence of power.

Add the power of Ten, the Higher Self, to the 6, the Present and the Presence, our history and our ancestors, and we have Avatars - Master Shamans/'People of Knowledge'. Those ancestors who became Masters of Energy, who found 'enlightenment' - the 'Great Joke of Life' - while alive in a human body.

To be a 16 means to be beyond little ego, to have melted self into unity with All-That-Is. This means from a human standpoint that 'I' is no longer individual but is felt from the perspective of All-Humans.

For us more ordinary mortals, the 16 is about surpassing our past, erasing our personal history and its effects upon the present, cleaning the slate of old negativity. Living with a clean past opens up the cosmic power of synchronicity and what passes as 'coincidence'. It opens us up to be awake for the cosmic nudges that come our way all the time but which, mostly, we manage to edit out of our experience by living preoccupied with the fantasy stories we tell ourselves.

16 is 1 and 6 which = 7 One who is Dancing The Dream Awake.

16 is 15 + 1. A soul who is gaining enlightenment.

16 is 7 + 9. A dreamer who knows right choreography of energy-movement, right choice.

16 is 8 + 8. One who has accepted their karma, learned their lessons and has open access to their Book of Life.

17. ARCHETYPAL ENERGIES. Weavers of the dream that is life on earth. Kachina-hey, gods, goddesses, archangels.

Add the Ten power of consciousness to the Seven of The Dream and we have Sacred Teachers of the Dream, the non-manifest beings who teach us in the dream world, who guide us when we are in quiet, un-busy, relaxed, meditative states, who hear our prayers, especially when they are truly heartfelt. These are the Spirit-Beings who guide the unfoldment of the dream that we experience as 'real life'.

This is the place of the Archetypal Energies as represented by the many gods such as the Greek pantheon or the Orisas of the Afro-Brazilian traditions. The Major Arcana of the Tarot is another map of archetypes. The Christian angels and archangels, Sisters of Wyrd of the Anglo-Saxon tradition, who eternally weave the fabric of the Universe, the Hopi Kachinas, even the Knights of the Round Table, are representations of these energies.

(Note: There is no essential difference between monotheistic and pantheistic cultures in the true sense of those words. All pantheistic cultures are monotheistic underneath in that they hold **All-That-Is** as all that is! All other arguments are anthropological error, mistaking of the ground of understanding of the Ancients, and come from looking at 'round' cultures through the 'square window' of Western literalist Christianised thinking. True monotheism means the Oneness of All-That-Is – the ultimate Unity of All Existence, nothing to do with a Big-Daddy-God-Chap Father-Christmas figure invented in the image of a human!)

For us, 17 is the place of our higher conscious dreams, imaginations, symbols, creations of the mind prior to manifestation in external reality. Our ability to imagine (I - the - Mage), to creatively dream, and thus the potential to manifest our dreams into three dimensional reality.

17 is 9 + 8. The Sacred teachers know and understand Design & Choreography Of Energy (9) according to Sacred Law (8).

17 is 12 + 5. Humans (5) who have fully awakened inner and outer connections to the Everything of the Earth (12) touch into archetypal consciousness (17). This relates to 'channeling' when one's voice is guided by a Spirit Being, and to psychic surgery when a Spirit-Doctor performs a healing using the hands of a mortal. It relates to 'possession' states where an archetypal energy enters and acts through us for a period. It is such a beautiful state of Oneness with a Great Being, and sadly our culture, through lack of understanding, is largely afraid of it. Of course, it has to be done only with clearest intention of working for the highest good of all.

17 = 1 and 7 = 8. Sacred teachers – and we can call them Archangels - bring us knowledge of laws of pattern, cycles of nature.

18. Absolute balance and justice. Karma Masters. Keepers of the Akashic Records. Our Book Of Life

Add the power of 10 to the 8 and we have the Akashic Records which contain our individual Book of Life, looked after by the Karma Masters, keepers of Sacred Law. These are the beings or energies who make and hold the laws of patterns and cycles at the highest level, the laws of how the Universe works, how all the energy is held in patterns to create observable, experienceable 'reality', who keep 'karma', the balance of all things, and thus the ultimate Absolute Justice of the Universe.

For us, 18 is about cleaning up the mind. Letting go of all those personal laws and rules of how we have been taught things are and how we think they 'should be', and tuning into Universal Mind and Sacred Law. The Buddhists call it 'Beginners Mind' or 'Unobstructed Awareness'. The ability to act without creating negative reaction (karma). And the ability to embody 'dreams' with such intent and focus that they just have to become manifest in third dimensional reality.

18 is 9 + 9. Understanding and knowledge of design of energy in both the Tonal (everyday) and Nagual (spiritual) realities.

18 is the place of Magick, the capability to master change. Add 8 - the knowledge of cycles, circles, and law, to 10 - higher consciousness. All images within form reflect our deepest concepts about how things are. Hence, if you want to change external reality, work on your deepest inner concepts.

18 is 10 plus 8. Our Higher Self (10) now knows how to open our Book of Life (8) and thus we can tune into Universal Mind and understand Cosmic Pattern.

19. Pure Science. Design of All-Existence. Goddess and God. Wakan and Ssquan - the Primal Feminine and Masculine Energies of the Universe.

Add Ten to Nine and we add higher consciousness to the power of design of energy movement and choice. The nineteen is the world of the Great Movers, the primal cosmic powers, the 'Gods and Goddesses' of the Universe. This is the place of Great Grandmother Wakan and Great Grandfather SSquan, the primal yin and yang. It is the Pure Science of the Universe, the design of all existence, the 'Mind of God'.

Living in constant contact with the highest, motivated for the Good-Of-All-Things, freely acting in concert with the Will of Great Spirit, truly living in the flow. The little self has died and the Great Self lives through us as an expression of Itself. Effortless Joyful Existence. The real meaning of the Biblical 'Resurrection'.

19 is 7, the Dream that is Life On Earth, plus 12 - all the Planets. Hence 19 relates to all life on all planets anywhere in the Universe.

20. All-That-Is. Great Mystery, Great Spirit, Creator God/Goddess, WakanTanka. (Wakan = holy, Tanka = a lot!)

Aluna, Allah, The Force, Tegashila, God, The Un-Nameable. The Great Tyrant.

Twenty is Great Mystery, The-Everything, made manifest in third dimensional reality. It is also completion and the potential of return to Zero. On this wheel Great Mystery / Great Spirit is placed in the West, the place of manifestation.

20 is 2 x 0, or 00 (double zero), infinity. We started this wheel with the 0 and we end with double 00. From no-thing to manifested no-thing!

Truly, we live in a wondrous World Of Dreams!

A STORY: A SPIRIT SEEKS INCARNATION
With a touch of humour....

The 19, Great Grandmother and Great Grandfather decide to send forth an aspect of themselves, an individual Spirit, to the Cosmic School of Planet Earth. An appointment is made with a Karma Master (18) to look into the Spirit's Book-Of-Life, stored in the Akashic Record.

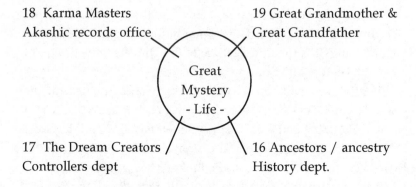

18 Karma Masters
Akashic records office

19 Great Grandmother &
Great Grandfather

Great
Mystery
- Life -

17 The Dream Creators
Controllers dept

16 Ancestors / ancestry
History dept.

The Spirit and the Karma Master meet. Together they examine what that particular Spirit-Being has learned so far and what its desires are for its next learning and how it wishes to contribute to the evolution of the whole. Perhaps the Spirit wishes to learn about how to live in peace and harmony with nurturing and loving relationships, so a good start for that might be a dysfunctional family living in a troubled place where revolution is simmering!

When this is all agreed upon, the Spirit's next appointment is with the Dream Controllers (17). They gaze into the 'dream' of life on earth and contact the archetypal energies ('gods') of war and peace, nurturing and standing-on-own-feet-somehow etc. The gods advise and a time and place for entry are chosen as most suitable.

Then the Spirit is sent to the History department (16) where the Ancestors seek a bloodline with appropriate heredity patterns and a suitable individual family who are in the throes of creating a new vehicle which will give the opportunity for a challenging, interesting and fruitful life experience....

> When the new vehicle (body) is prepared,
> the Spirit walks through the 'Veil of Forgetfulness',
> an absolute condition for earth incarnation,
> and joins the vehicle
> in the womb-cave
> until ready to emerge
> into the three dimensional

GREAT COSMIC TRAINING SCHOOL OF MOTHER EARTH,

and a new life begins!

A-Ho!

LIFE'S GREAT JOURNEY OF AWAKENING

All us humans travel the Great Journey of Awakening whether we perceive it, intend it, couldn't be bothered about it, just live for money-power-sex-indulgence and couldn't care less about it - or are seriously engaged in the endeavour to journey to a state of higher consciousness and experience a true state of unity with the cosmos! The whole boiling lot of us are on this journey together, consciously and unconsciously, and our ultimate destiny is collective and is part of the ultimate destiny of Planet Earth, of our Sun, of our Milky Way Galaxy and of the Whole Universe.

The journey has been described in many ways by many cultures and called by many names: The Perennial Philosophy, the Search for the Holy Grail, the Buddha's search for enlightenment, the lives of Mithras / Horus / Thammuz and the many other God-man legends, the Jesus Story as understood by the Gnostic Christians, the Arthurian legends, the Journey of Osiris/Dionysus, the Journey into the Mind of God, the Hero's Journey and so on. Here is the essence of the Journey mapped out by the teachings of the medicine wheel.

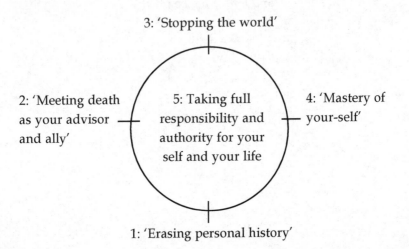

3: 'Stopping the world'

2: 'Meeting death as your advisor and ally'

5: Taking full responsibility and authority for your self and your life

4: 'Mastery of your-self'

1: 'Erasing personal history'

1. SOUTH

The first step is to the direction of the South and is called, with the humour of the Heyeokah, 'ERASING PERSONAL HISTORY'. Why humourously? Because it's not literally possible! To be more literal we can call it 'Embracing Personal History' or 'Healing The Inner Child'.

As we have talked about in many ways throughout this book, this step is about erasing the negative controlling effects from the past on the present. To work through the old traumas, fears, phobias, addictions, repressed anger, hate, resentment, grief, sadness, bitterness, loss, abandonments, betrayals, hurts, wounds and so on. This means to do whatever doctoring of the psyche is needed. From the Greek – psyche means soul, therapeia means doctoring - psycho-spiritual therapy work to doctor the soul.

The work is to heal the emotional body so that one becomes an actor in the world, not a re-actor. One gains mastery over the 'lower' self and is no longer run by the emotions, but is guided by feelings. Psychic abilities begin to open up as the confusing muddle of emotional needs, wants, and addictions retreat to the sidelines as defeated monsters that now become friends.

One very important point for Westerners.

EMOTIONAL HEALING HAS TWO DISTINCT STAGES.

1. GET IN TOUCH WITH FEELINGS.

Open up to the buried pain and anguish locked away in one's past, which for so many silently wreaks havoc with daily life, health and happiness. This is the painful work where the hurts of the past live on, hidden in the memory, in the body, until they are brought forth and released. In this way healing can take place.

2. DISCIPLINE THE EMOTIONS.

Only a child lives with uncontrolled emotions. Now it is time to gain control of the emotional body. To feel your feelings but to have control of when and how you express them, but, most importantly, without suppressing them.

A lot of problems are caused by a lack of understanding of these two distinct yet seemingly contradictory stages. Sometimes it seems that some spiritual paths teach only the second stage and some psychotherapy teaches only the first. This can lead to 'stiff upper lip' spiritual people and emotionally out of control therapees!

How others hold us in their image.
Erasing personal history has another vital aspect and that is how others hold us in their image of us. Our family and friends will have a firm idea of who we are, of our abilities and talents, our quirks and blindnesses. And, of course, they are also likely to have very strong opinions about just who we 'should' be.

Once we grow and change, we will no longer play the same 'pain games' with them. We talked about this in the section on the Warrior's Path but it needs repeating. These are battles that we must face and win.

All spiritual paths have coded instructions that deal with the problem of losing friends and family and how this may be inevitable, for a time. A person who has been a family scapegoat returns to the parental home after a time of growth and transition and all the old games are played out by the other family members, but now the person no longer reacts powerlessly. The result is likely to be fear and anger on the part of the family as they try to bring the returning one back into the familiar family system. This person is 'not the son (daughter, grandchild, sister, brother, husband, wife, etc.) that I knew' and what right have they to behave in this way? The Warrior must stand firm no matter what. If the price is losing friends and family, then so be it, things can always heal with time. To give in is to lose a Battle-of-the-Soul, and that battle will come up to be fought again and again. And each time it is likely to be more challenging.

CONTEMPLATIVE TRADITIONS.
The traditions of the contemplative, the monk and nun, the reclusive shaman up on the hill away from the tribe, the yogi

disciple at the ashram, these are all traditions which make a place to separate from one's previous life and thus serve to 'erase personal history'. By taking a new name, shaving one's hair or no longer cutting it, living alone or in a separate community with others on a similar path, dedicating one's whole life to totally different pursuits than before, one effectively breaks the chain from the past and creates an opportunity to re-invent oneself.

On the Medicine Wheel:-

This movement is a joining of the South to the Southeast power. Through healing of the 'wounded child' aspect of our-self we change (erase) the hold our history has had on us and we heal the legacy of our ancestors, thus energetically freeing them. In doing that we also free our descendents as the negative energy no longer travels forward to them.

DROPPING YOUR PAST AT A STROKE AND LIVING IN THE NOW (1)
THE VIEW FROM THE INNER CHILD.

A number of popular books have been published in the last few years suggesting we can (should?) just let go of the past and its traumas and live in the now. It's a great idea! It is where all of us on the path are ultimately trying to go - to be free of baggage and to walk lightly on the earth unencumbered by old wounds. How fabulous just to be able to let go at a stroke and move on, free of childhood traumas, influences from the past, emotional blindness that lingers on from incompleted life cycles, free of leftover puberty confusions from the total lack of intelligent puberty rites in our culture, everyone and everything who ever did anything against us in the past completely forgiven, all negative energy released, vanquished, nullified. Great!

It is just that I have never met anyone who has done so like that. It is a great idea to be able just to drop it all but my experience with myself over thirty years is that I have had to recapitulate each piece in order to be truly free of it. I have had to enter the place of the inner child where the energy is stored and re-experience it in order to release it properly so it doesn't linger on to reappear when I am trying to look the other way. I have had to let my inner child have his say, express his feelings and, when appropriate, scream and shout. Only then has change happened. I, the adult, through honouring the child instead of ignoring him as is so easy to do, gave him the time be heard, to be vindicated, and to release his pain.

The idea that people can just let go of years of stuck pain and trauma in a painless moment is nonsense and what concerns me is that the idea of dropping it all at a stroke could become yet another New Age 'right way to be' and just another way to deny the truth of a painful past and ignore its effects on the present. Wouldn't we all like a nice painless way of healing ourselves? All who have entered the real path of self-healing and self-development know it is a challenging and humbling road - humbling especially. If there is one thing we don't need it is another comfortable excuse to avoid and deny the truth.

Ordinary world requirements: Healing the inner child by whatever means works for you

Spirit world requirements: Daring to live with trust in the Universe from a place of innocence - so you come to live in a magical world.

2. WEST

The second stage of the Journey is the West and the name given to this stage is 'MEETING DEATH AS AN ADVISOR AND ALLY'. This has many meanings starting with the basic one of re-membering at a deep fundamental level that the body we inhabit is temporary and will one day be claimed by Death. That means that this incarnate journey ends, not that we end as consciousness. This opportunity for growth and development here in flesh on the Great Mother living enmeshed in the material world between the forces of light, dark and shadow comes to an end. We go back to the Great Round, to the Spirit World from which we came at birth.

It also means facing the need for pieces of ourselves to die. Death gives life. The living person who is 'dead' has not allowed their redundant bits and pieces of self to die, has resisted change.

We all know someone like that, someone who is stuck and miserable and defeatist. They are emotionally constipated, hanging on to all their old baggage. The only thing that is constant in this Earth reality is change and when we resist it we get stuck and go 'dead' - ultimately into depression.

The quality of the West is introspection, self knowledge. Self knowledge leads to knowledge of all selves, of the race. The West is also about collective issues. We are not islands, we are part of our family, village, tribe, city, country and ultimately all humanity and all of Planet Earth.

Many experiments have been done with groups of meditators getting together to intend peacefulness with the result that crime rates in the area have been proved to be reduced. Quoted in the movie 'What he bleep do we know' is one such study conducted in the USA's crime capital, Washington DC. At the end of the study, it was demonstrated that the crime rate had reduced – for that period at any rate - by the astonishing figure of 25%.

When we introspect deeply we touch into the archetypal world and we can begin to see what forces are playing out through us. With a deep inner world connection, our intuition grows. Intuition is connection with the Spirit world or realm of cause. It is the state of consciousness where we can 'know' things and dispense with believing what others would have us believe. Thus we move forward on our journey to self-determination and individuation and we become contributors to the evolution of all.

On the MEDICINE WHEEL:

This movement is a joining of the West and the Southwest. The quality of deep introspection is the quality of effective *dreaming*. The ability to *dream* one's intent so clearly that it will manifest into the material world.

Ordinary world requirement: Goal setting - clear goals - achievable - worthwhile - will make you feel really good about yourself and your life.

Spirit world requirement: To touch spirit's dream (goal) for you in this incarnation.

3. NORTH

The third direction of the journey is the North, the realm of the mind, and here the movement is called 'STOPPING THE WORLD' or 'DIRECT KNOWING' or 'UNOBSTRUCTED AWARENESS'. This means stopping the busy-mind everyday trance state of normal waking consciousness that tells us that the world is 'out there' and is happening to us. By 'Stopping The World', we contact the inner realm of cause, of Spirit, which shows us that is where it all really happens and that the outer world is but an echo, a reflection.

On the MEDICINE WHEEL:

The movement to the North is a joining with the Northwest powers. This is a bringing together of knowledge and under-standing of the patterned nature of reality, of cosmic law and of ultimate absolute justice and balance. We open our mind power to the knowledge of how the Universe really works.

DROPPING YOUR PAST AT A STROKE AND LIVING IN THE
NOW (2)
THE VIEW FROM THE ADULT.

When we travel the journey around the Wheel and get to the North we will be ready to 'Stop The World', drop baggage and live in the here-and-now. This is when the 'living-in-the-now' books can be appropriate and very helpful.

I remember an old Irish joke. "Can you tell me the way to Dublin?" says English car driver, lost in the outer reaches of Irish countryside, to local yokel. Yokel scratches head looking deeply puzzled. "Aye, but if I was you I wouldn't start from here".

That's the problem - we can't get there - the here and now - the 'other side of the North' - until we have fully travelled the South and the West. To get to the enlightened place of living in the present unencumbered by anxieties of past and future, we have to GO THROUGH THE PROCESS of recapitulation of our life to whatever extent we need to, which is individual for each of us.

This is our apprenticeship and there is no shortcut, however attractive it can seem. If a book tells you that you should just drop your past and be-here-now - and it doesn't seem to be working for you - there is nothing wrong with you, it is just too early in your journey for that book. I am reminded of the British comedian Larry Grayson who, back in the 60's, seemed to appear from nowhere and became a headliner with his own show in almost no time. "I was an overnight success in 25 years" he quipped. He had served a full apprenticeship, years of treading the boards of countless small clubs around the country. When his opportunity came his skills were honed, he was ready for it, and he grasped it with both hands.

Every stage of life needs its due, in time, effort, intensity - and humility. There are no shortcuts, whatever anyone tells you.

Ordinary world requirement: To live as a wise adult

Spirit world requirement: To stop the world, be fully here-now, and 'see' the energy of the world beyond merely the five senses.

4. EAST

The fourth movement is to the East and is called 'MASTERING THE DREAM', subtitled 'SEEKING VISION AND PURPOSE'. To be a master in the everyday realm means to master the 'dream' realm, the inner world of spirit, of intent (thought), emotion (energy-motion), of introspection (inner knowing of one's earth-self), of imagination (magical knowing of one's spirit self).

Now we quest for vision and seek direct connection with the causal realm and our spirit teachers to clarify our deepest intent for this life so we can *'dance the dream awake'*. It is time to dare to awaken to true reality.

WHO IS BOSS?

The issue of who is Boss of our Ship-of-Self is a very big one as our culture teaches us to have the mind in control at all times. The price of this is that we rarely get beyond the thinking, calculating place that is constantly looking to the future, avoiding experiencing the now. Mind is a savage boss but a good servant. So now we ally our design of life, our power of choice, with Spirit, and relegate mind to its rightful place as advisor.

On the MEDICINE WHEEL:

This movement is a joining of the East with the Northeast, of the place of eagle and vision with the place of choice and design of energy. We choose mastery, we choose to be conscious rather than asleep, we choose to connect the fifth dimension of the 'dream' with the manifest realm of the third. We choose focus our full intent on self-mastery.

Ordinary world requirement: To master your human vehicle and its addictions. To manifest your life-dreams that you set as goals.

Spirit world requirement: To unite your life-dream with that of Creator and thus serve the Evolution of Creation

5. CENTRE.

The last movement is to the Centre and this means taking on full responsibility for our existence and stepping into a place of True Personal Power. With no more personal history, there is nothing and no one to blame. We take full responsibility for all our actions. Life is a perfect balance of light and dark, an arena for playing, learning and growing into illumination and enlightenment, guided by Spirit, living in trust and innocence, a child again but this time a Magical Child-Adult Integrated Whole Being.

Ordinary world requirement: Done

Spirit world requirement: To serve the evolution of all beings.

BECOMING THE SHAMAN
MASTERING THE WHEEL OF LIFE
'Getting down off the cross'

The sign of the shaman, one who has 'got off their cross' and
mastered their wheel of life, is shown by the sign below.

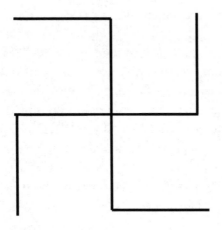

SUMMARISING THE GREAT JOURNEY

1. 'Erasing personal history', healing the past, is the joining of the
South to the Southeast. The 'wounded child' is healed by full
acceptance of one's ancestry and history without blame, shame or
guilt. Negative effects from the past are erased by complete
unconditional acceptance of how it was, why it was, what it was.
All enemies and petty tyrants now become teachers along life's
road. Letting go of the baggage with its hurts of the past and
expectations for the future leaves a person free to be their true self,
fully present, right here and now, with all their energy available.

2. As we join the West to the Southwest we consciously become the
co-creator of our own 'dream' of life as well as the experiencer.
Now we have 'Danced our Dream Awake'. We accept that the
enemy is old age, inertia and finally death and we let death be our
advisor for living to the fullest while we are alive.

This doesn't mean life is necessarily easy because there are other people's dreams, and maybe some very unaware ones, impinging on our own. But it means we are free to respond with full conscious intent and focus, without the weight of baggage and the power loss of addictions. We have great power to affect the moment and the maturity to accept it as it is. It will mean that from the perspective of those who seek to be in control, one is now quite likely to be seen as an anarchist!

3. The joining of the North to the Northwest. This means acceptance of karma, the lessons we are here to learn, and the freeing of the mind from its anxieties about the future. In the end we are all dead! From this point of view there is no future, there is only the Eternal Present, so – quite literally - NOTHING MATTERS. (A very profound statement - think about it in the light of shamanic teaching and quantum physics!) Now the world can be 'stopped' and the mind becomes free to be fully conscious here and now in multi-dimensional awareness.

4. The joining of the East to the Northeast means to unite one's choices with those of Spirit. One joins one's own personal 'Dream of Life' with the 'Dream' of All-Creation. The separated illusory ego dies and the Self is (re)born in Love, Light and Truth. The crucifixion and the awakening. The separated ego is dead and the true self is awakened.

The journey from apprentice to shaman is complete, though it is never ending. The ego has to keep on dying, the true-self has to keep on manifesting. While we are alive in a body, the challenges go on and on every moment.......... We do not so much '*get down of the cross*' as live with it and beyond it at the same time.

Living from Centre means that one no longer exists as a separate ego-identity but as part of All-That-Exists. One is a vehicle through which spirit - creation - god expresses its Self. As one is no longer an individual self and no longer burdened with self-concepts, one no longer has anything to defend, anything to try, anything to achieve, anything to prove! Such a relaxation, such ease, such a saving of energy!

AND NOTHING TO BELIEVE - what a relief!

Ah, but that includes everything in this book too - none of this for believing either - it is maps and concepts to help you 'see' and feel for yourself and to navigate yourself through your life. Life, Itself, is The Road.

May the Medicine Wheel guide and help you to find
Balance and Harmony, Humour and Humility,
wherever you travel.

May you Walk a Good Road, Walk your Talk and
Touch the World in Beauty in the Great Vision Quest
of Life. A-Ho!

There comes the time when we are naturally ready to give back.......

A MEDICINE WHEEL OF HELPING OTHERS

2. GIVE THEM TOOLS
TO HELP THEMSELVES

3. TEACH THEM
HOW TO USE
THE TOOLS
AND HELP
FEED
THEMSELVES

5. THEY FEED
THEMSELVES
AND RETURN TO
SHOW YOU A NEW
AND BETTER WAY

4. TAKE THEM
HUNTING,
TEACH THEM
WHAT YOU
KNOW

1. FEED THE HUNGRY

All who follow the path of self-healing become healers for others. It may not be professionally but as a person heals inside, others will instinctively seek them out as a source of help and guidance. Here is a map of the natural progression of helping.

Let us turn this metaphor to the subject of PERSONAL DEVELOPMENT:-

1. ONE TO ONE SESSIONS, BEGINNERS WORKSHOPS. Help the people to heal, take the needy through the underworld to experience the hidden and rejected parts of themselves, help them retrieve lost soul parts and start to live more fully.

2.. MORE ADVANCED WORKSHOPS AND SESSIONS. Teach them the tools for self-understanding, self-development, self-awareness, self-love, self-fulfillment. Give them practices to do on their own.

3. TRAINING COURSES. Teach them how to use the tools to retrieve their own and each other's lost parts, to become more self-sufficient in their own development, to be guides for themselves on their journey so they can become guides and helpers for others.

4. MAKE THEM YOUR ASSISTANT LEADERS. Give them the opportunity to take responsibility and to 'give away' their knowledge and understanding to others, to learn by experience, while you are there to assist and guide.

5. THEY SET UP THEIR OWN WORKSHOPS / SESSIONS. All good students are expected to ultimately exceed the teacher! They come back and show you the new things they have discovered. THE CIRCLE IS COMPLETE.

AFTERWORD

The Medicine Wheel maps out the world from the greatest to the smallest and gives us clues as to who we are, where we come from, why we are here, where we can go and what we are here to learn.

The local workings of Great-Mystery-God can be observed at all times by watching nature, seeing the natural world and how it lives. By watching the growth and decay in the garden that occurs with the seasons and nature's feeding and reproduction cycles, you are observing the actions of the Great Mother and her Kingdoms which are the close-to-us part of Great-Mystery-God. By observing the planets, the stars, the galaxy and the interactions that go on in the heavens, you are seeing the grand workings of Great-Mystery-God. Quantum physics and the strange non-linear and seemingly non-logical things that happen at the level of the incredibly small show us the inner workings of Great-Mystery-God and how consciousness is formed into the incredible matrix that we experience as everyday life.

The shamans and elders of ancient cultures – our ancestors - learned through observation. They didn't set out a load of beliefs and force people to follow them, they studied how things are and learned from nature by observing, by trial and error, by experience. They knew that the Universe is a Wholeness and that nothing exists outside it, so to them the idea of a big-daddy-god who resides external to 'his' Creation is nothing short of absurd, rather like a Father Christmas / Santa Claus figure for people who don't want to grow up!

Many amazing experiments have been conducted in the realm of Quantum Physics that suggest that at the hidden level of the incredibly small there is no distance and no time as we know it; that no actual substance exists at all but everything is formed of energy waves and vortexes; that everything is interconnected so there can be no such thing as a purely objective observer; that our DNA, even if removed and far away, remains forever connected to our living body (hence the strange effects of transplants on their recipients); that there is a field of energy (often dubbed the 'Zero Point Field') that is not visible to the eye but is everywhere around and within us and through which everything is connected. This is the world as seen by the shamans of old, long before 'scientific proof' was deemed necessary and science was constrained by the mechanics we have available to 'prove' anything.

Within this field are all future possibilities and it is through our interaction with this field via our beliefs, emotions, mental structures and prayers, that one of these possibilities comes to be manifested into the 'reality' we experience. Hence the enormous importance of what we believe, how we feel and think, and what we pray for, both consciously and unconsciously. We may think we are praying for something, calling something nice into our lives but if we believe deep down that we are not worth it, something quite different will manifest reflecting our neurotic beliefs. It is what is hidden deep in the unconscious that affects most what comes to be and hence the enormous importance of healing our personal history so that old pains, hurts and resentments no longer linger hidden away.

By stalking our inner power - our integrity, authenticity, wisdom, ability to love, self-regard; by forgiving and releasing wounds of the past, by mastering our responses to our karma-life-lessons, by dreaming a good dream that benefits all beings, we can design and choreograph a life of joy. Perhaps joyful challenge is more accurate as the challenges don't stop!

Putting this in terms of the Medicine Wheel: –

Our challenge is –

to raise our 6 (our self-concepts) by 'erasing' our personal history so we move towards becoming the 16, the (en)lightened human, a person of light, unencumbered by past;

to raise our 7, the 'dreamer' who desires, visualises and prays for the life sought, towards 17, an aspect of Great-Dreamer whose dream is part of the dream of All-That-Is;

to raise our 8, our internalised patterns which run us until we master them, towards 18, mastery of our patterns and our karma, able to live in harmony, balance and justice;

to raise our 9, the individual decision maker / goal seeker towards the 19, the ultimate decision maker, Great-Mystery-God, bringing our-self and our life into harmony with Creation.

These are the things to work towards so we can come to truly value our selves, our sister and brother humans, our lives, our planetary home and its multitude of beings, and our full place in the Universe.

The challenge is none less than – as a species - to grow up or die.

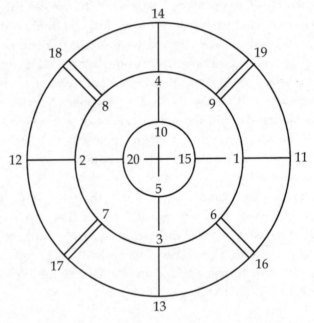

Many old cultures have myths that say this is the third world or the fourth world and it may soon end. Some say this is the stage at which former humanities destroyed themselves or were destroyed and had to start over again from just a few survivors.

We have the weapons of mass destruction, the bombs, the pollution, the poisons and climate change. All that we need to really take it out on ourselves is ready, primed and waiting. We can become the paranoid schizophrenic who trusts no one but himself and must eradicate all other in order to feel safe and secure.....

OR WE CAN GROW UP...

Growing up means REAL-ising that there is only One Hu-Man Being and we are all cells in the one body of Hu-Man = 'Divine-Mortal'.

> Each of us is a Wave in the Ocean of Creation.
> What we do to others we do to ourselves.
> Instead of asking 'What can I get out of it?'
> Ask 'What can I give?
> What does Creation ask from me?'
> Growing up means compassion for all beings;
> No more blaming 'other', no more bombs;
> Self love means love for all selves,
> Compassion and respect for all beings;
> Sharing the fruits of the earth, our mother;
> Co-operation, not humanity-defeating competition.

> 'Self'-realisation ultimately means no more 'me'!

> It's not too late
> But it's nearly too late
> IT'S TIME TO WAKE UP!

And so we spiral back to the direction in which we started: -

IN THE BEGINNING IS GREAT GRANDMOTHER WAKAN
THE 'GREAT ROUND'

CREATION IS THE JOINING OF
GREAT GRANDMOTHER WAKAN
AND GREAT GRANDFATHER SSQUAN

GREAT GRANDFATHER, THE SPARK OF LIGHT,

IS PENETRATING GREAT GRANDMOTHER, THE SEED, THE
EGG,
IN MIGHTY ORGASM,

CREATING THE UNIVERSE
OF YIN AND YANG,
FEMININE AND MASCULINE -

CREATION IS TAKING PLACE ..

CONSTANTLY...

CREATOR IS EXPERIENCING
IT'S SELF -

- IN DIVERSITY AND

MULTIPLICITY

ALL IS ONE....

FROM THE ONE IS
COMING -

ALL-THAT-IS

HERE WE ARE

BIBLIOGRAPHY.

By the same author
(Thorsons) WAY OF SHAMANISM. Thorsons 2001
(Previously published as 'Principles of shamanism'. Thorsons 1996
SHAMANIC PATH WORKBOOK. Arima publications 2006
(Previous version published by Piatkus 2001)
SOUL COMPANIONS by Karen Sawyer. O-Books 2008.
Compilation includes chapter by Leo Rutherford
ADAM & EVIL: THE 'GOD' WHO HATES SEX, WOMEN AND
HUMAN BODIES. By The Heyeokah Guru. Dandelion Books, USA
/ Trafford Publications UK 2007

Other authors:
LIGHTNINGBOLT   by Hyemeyohsts Storm. Ballantine 1994
SEVEN ARROWS   by Hyemeyohsts Storm.   Ballantine 1972
SECRETS OF SHAMANISM: Tapping the spirit power within you.
by Jose Stevens and Lena S. Stevens. Harper Collins 1988
THE POWER PATH: The Shaman's Way to Success in Business and
Life by Jose Stevens & Lena Stevens   New World Library 2002
NEW PSYCHO-CYBERNETICS by Maxwell Maltz.   Penguin
Puttnam 2001
The CONTINUUM CONCEPT: In Search of Happiness Lost. By
Jean Liedloff. Perseus Books 1977
THE MAKING OF THEM by Nick Duffell.   Lone Arrow Press,
London N8 7LP.   2000
SHAMANIC VOICES by Joan Halifax. Arkana1992
THE MEDICINE WAY by Kenneth Meadows. Element Books 1990
SHAMANIC HEALING within the medicine wheel by Marie-Lu
Lorler. Brotherhood of Life 1989
THE NEW PHYSICS OF CONSCIOUSNESS by David Ash. 2007
MAPS TO ECSTASY: The Healing Power of Movement
by Gabrielle Roth and John Loudon. New World Library 1998
THE TURNING POINT.   By Fritjof Capra. Flamingo 1983
THE JESUS MYSTERIES   by Timothy Freke and Peter Gandy.
Thorsons 1999

RESOURCES

Eagle's Wing Centre for Contemporary Shamanism,
Box BCM 7475, London WC1N 3XX. UK 01435-810233
www.shamanism.co.uk (Founded by the author, 1987)
Society for Shamanic Practitioners UK, c/o Elsa and Howard
Malpas, 42 The Grove, Isleworth, Middx, TW7 4JF. 020-758-9950
Sacred Hoop Magazine (UK shamanism magazine),
Anghorfa, Abercych, Boncath, Pembrokeshire, SA37 0EZ   01239-
682029 www.sacredhoop.org
Celebrating Woman, www.celebratingwoman.co.uk / 01435-
810308 / BCM Box 7475, London WC1N 3XX, UK. Shamanic
workshops for women.
Shamanic Warrior, Elsa and Howard Malpas, c/o Isle of Avalon
foundation, 2-4 High Street, Glastonbury, Somerset, BA6 9 DU, UK
020-758-9950. http://www.shamanicwarrior.com
N'Goma Kundi (Shamanic) Drummers
Doug Blacksmith, 7 Martindale, East Sheen, SW14 7AL, UK   020-
8876-0979
Spirit Horse Nomadic Circle, PO Box 66, Llandrindod. LD1 9AH,
UK 07882-522878.   www.spirithorse.co.uk
The Sacred Trust, PO Box 7777, Wimborne, Dorset, BH21 9DJ, UK
mail@sacredtrust.co.uk Tel: (+44) 01258 840392
Deer Tribe Medicine Society UK: 01246-415658 / www.singing-
stones.org / wocy@greenmesa.free-online.co.uk
USA: Harley Swiftdeer Reagan. http://www.dtmms.org
Ehama Institute UK.
http://www.thejourneytree.org/ehama/index.htm
Joan Halifax Roshi, Upaya Zen Center, 1404 Cerro Gordo Road,
Santa Fe, NM, 7501. UAS. Phone: 505-986-8518, Fax: 505-986-8528,
Email: upaya@upaya.org
Trackways – Wild craft, survival, wilderness spirit courses in UK.
www.trackways.co.uk / 01273-480429